UNSOLVED MYSTERIES OF THE OLD WEST

UNSOLVED MYSTERIES OF THE OLD WEST

Second Edition

W. C. Jameson

TAYLOR TRADE PUBLISHING
Lanham • New York • Boulder • Toronto • Plymouth, UK

Published by Taylor Trade Publishing
An imprint of The Rowman & Littlefield Publishing Group, Inc.
4501 Forbes Boulevard, Suite 200, Lanham, Maryland 20706
www.rowman.com

10 Thornbury Road, Plymouth PL6 7PP, United Kingdom

Distributed by National Book Network

British Library Cataloguing in Publication Information Available

Library of Congress Cataloging-in-Publication Data

Jameson, W.C., 1942-
  Unsolved mysteries of the old West / W.C. Jameson. — Second edition.
    pages cm
  Includes bibliographical references.
  ISBN 978-1-58979-741-3 (pbk. : alk. paper) — ISBN 978-1-58979-742-0
(electronic) 1. West (U.S.)—History—Miscellanea. 2. West (U.S.)—Biography—
Miscellanea. I. Title.
  F591.J38 2013
  978—dc23

                                                        2012042514

∞™ The paper used in this publication meets the minimum requirements of American National Standard for Information Sciences—Permanence of Paper for Printed Library Materials, ANSI/NISO Z39.48-1992.

Printed in the United States of America

Contents

Introduction

・◆・

Most observers of human culture and society in America have long
been aware of the notion that there are two things that people
continue to be fascinated by: the Old West and a good mystery.

No one can deny the enduring attraction and mystique of the frontier American West, a geographic and cultural region that has yielded
indelible images of outlaws, lawmen, gunfights, train robberies, wagon
trains, trail drives, settlements, gold mining, and more. Though fic-
tionalized, fantasized, glorified, and mythologized via film, novels,
and song, these images continue to provide us with adventure, excitement, romance, and mystery.

A number of Western events and personalities have yielded some of
America's most elusive mysteries. Because of a variety of factors, the
life, death, and times of many famous Western figures are fraught with
contradiction. Huge gaps exist in the knowledge and information pertaining to them. In addition to people, places and things also provide
compelling mysteries.

With the passage of time, the images of some Western personalities
have actually evolved from bad men to heroes. Real-life crimes ranging from horse rustling to murder are often obscured by the outlaw's
contemporary and overriding image, a persona that has sometimes
been reshaped such that it bears little or no relationship to truth and
reality. Outlaws of yore are oftentimes re-created, not as the bad men
they actually were, but as rebellious and individualistic souls who
have been misunderstood and persecuted by law enforcement authorities. Today, many criminals of yesteryear are viewed by the public as
merely rule-breaking free spirits who had to contend with crooked
capitalists and corrupt politicians. The outlaw of the Old West, along
with some Western lawmen and other figures have, in truth, become
folk heroes in American and world society. In the process, much of the
truth of their lives and deaths remains unknown or misunderstood.

Mysteries, like the people, places, and things of the Old West, are likewise compelling. Particularly intriguing are those mysteries that have never been solved. On a global scale, there exist several prevailing unsolved mysteries that continue to fascinate, baffle, perplex, taunt, and entertain. Examples include the Loch Ness Monster, Bigfoot, the Bermuda Triangle, Unidentified Flying Objects, and the hypothesized existence of Noah's ark atop Turkey's Mount Ararat.

The serious investigator of Western American history encounters an array of mysteries as compelling and baffling as those listed above, accounts replete with conundrums, loose ends, and examples of twisted logic and truth. The more one immerses oneself in the details of the life, times, and deaths of notable figures such as Billy the Kid, Pat Garrett, Butch Cassidy, Etta Place, Belle Starr, John Wilkes Booth, Colonel Albert Jennings Fountain, and others, the more one grows keenly aware of the reasons why these and other cases remain mysterious and unsolved.

For one thing, many Western figures, including outlaws, lawmen, and even some politicians, led somewhat clandestine lives and commonly suppressed knowledge and information pertinent to their backgrounds and activities. Men and women sometimes arrived in the American West as a result of escaping complications, legal and otherwise, encountered elsewhere. In so doing, the newcomers often invented fresh backgrounds for themselves and in many cases assumed different names. Their lives were sometimes so cryptic or camouflaged that they left behind little or nothing helpful to researchers who followed decades later.

For another thing, the newspaper reporting during the early settlement times in the American West, when and if it occurred at all, was often spotty, inaccurate, biased, and often politically motivated. Additionally, since the deaths of noted Western figures, subsequent research on them has, in far too many cases, been sloppy and amateurish which has often only served to obscure, rather than reveal, the truth.

To further complicate matters, a lot of America's Western history, and in particular Western outlaw and lawman history, is sometimes treated as little more than an intellectual stepchild among serious scholars of American history. Western outlaws and lawman history is seldom provided much, if any, attention by credentialed and qualified researchers, many of whom are employed by colleges and universities. Academic departments generally encourage their professors to' undertake research into areas deemed to have greater import, research pertaining to major influences on shaping the history of America, and research that has the potential to attract significant grants. The academic reward system is based, in large part, on such things. As a result, a great deal of the history of the American West is neglected by the very people who should be concerned about it.

Many of those who pursue the study of this kind of history tend to be enthusiasts or hobbyists. Though committed, and occasionally qualified, many of them lack proper research and investigative credentials and experience. As a result they often wind up being responsible for clouding issues rather than clearing them up. However pure their motives and sincere their efforts, they are often guilty of simply copying and repeating what has already been written, much of which has long since been proven to be inaccurate. Rather than solve the mysteries that have puzzled folks for so long, they actually perpetuate them. Manifest in a lot of research oriented toward America's Western history today is a bias for maintaining the status quo, and a kind of reverence for things as they are perceived but not necessarily as they really were.

In this book the reader encounters twenty-two of the Old West's most baffling mysteries, those that continue to lure the curious and beg for investigation. The solutions to these mysteries, however, have eluded experts for generations.

The life and times of Billy the Kid offer one such mystery. Was this enigmatic outlaw actually gunned down in Fort Sumner, New Mexico, in 1881 by Sheriff Pat Garrett, or did he survive and go on to live a long life in hiding? Many writers contend the Kid was killed by Garrett, but critical and in-depth investigation suggests otherwise. Even Pat Garrett himself was slain under mysterious circumstances, and his murderer is no closer to being identified today than he was over a century ago.

Closely linked to Billy the Kid and Pat Garrett was Colonel Albert Jennings Fountain, a noted soldier, lawyer, and politician. Fountain disappeared with his son, Henry, under a cloud of mystery, and to this day has never been found. This nationally prominent case likewise remains unsolved.

The deaths and disappearances of Tombstone bad men Johnny Ringo, Buckskin Frank Leslie, and the Catalina Kid, as well as Warren Earp, have never been solved, and the fate of these men continues to generate discussion and debate even today. Similarly, the disappearance of female outlaw Pearl Hart and the death of her counterpart Belle Starr have never been solved.

Texas gunmen Bill Longley and John Wesley Hardin also provide interesting cases. Officially, Longley was hanged for murder, but family and friends maintained he fled and lived a long and successful life in Louisiana. There is no question that Hardin was killed by El Paso, Texas, constable John Selman, an act witnessed by several onlookers. The circumstances of the killing, however, have never been clear.

A growing number of researchers are convinced John Wilkes Booth, the assassin of President Abraham Lincoln, escaped from federal authorities and died nearly forty years later as a result of suicide in El Reno, Oklahoma.

Though their stories have been told many times, the disappearances and deaths of outlaws Black Bart, Butch Cassidy, and Kid Curry remain in question today.

According to research, the severed head of noted Mexican bandit and revolutionary war general Pancho Villa is hidden somewhere in the United States.

In addition to the aforementioned figures, the American West is replete with tales and legends of lost mines and buried treasures, much of which has never been recovered. The locations of these mines and caches have been sought, in some cases, for centuries, but many of their secrets remain elusive.

Yet another intriguing mystery is that of the so-called "thunderbird," which played a major role in American Indian culture. Did such a creature actually exist? While many consign this bird to the realm of mythology, recently discovered evidence suggests that it may have existed.

In writing a book such as this, it is my hope that many of these Unsolved Mysteries of the Old West serve to stimulate interest and additional research and investigation into the various cases. Adventure aplenty can be found in pursuing these subjects. If one is patient and committed, perhaps additional truths can be discovered. And what is the study of history if not a search for the truth.

ONE

✦✦✦

The Mysterious "Death" of Billy the Kid

One of the most famous shootings in the American West occurred around midnight on July 14, 1881, in Fort Sumner, New Mexico. It not only became one of the most baffling events of all time, it initiated the beginning of one of the most controversial issues and greatest mysteries in Western outlaw history.

That evening, according to many history books, Sheriff Pat Garrett shot and killed the notorious outlaw Billy the Kid in the bedroom of rancher Pete Maxwell. The Kid had escaped from the Lincoln County jail while awaiting execution, a sentence imposed on him following his conviction in the murder of a lawman. As more and more information has become available over the years, however, and as the events of that evening are examined in detail, it becomes clear that the history books have been wrong.

During the past century, an impressive amount of evidence has accumulated suggesting that Billy the Kid was never killed by Garrett, and that he lived for another sixty-nine years, outliving the sheriff and virtually everyone else involved in the Lincoln County War.

Billy the Kid, though colorful and legendary, may have been one of the most overrated outlaws in the history of the American West. Stealing cattle and horses was what the Kid was good at, but as rustlers go he was a small-time operator. Billy the Kid has been credited by some for killing as many as twenty-one men, one for each year of his life. The truth remains, however, that it is difficult to find evidence that he killed more than four or five, and even some of those are questionable. The Kid was sentenced to hang for the killing of Sheriff William Brady on April 1, 1878, a crime of which he may have been innocent.

Before he could be led to the gallows, the Kid escaped from the Lincoln County jail on April 28, 1881, killing two deputies in the process.

Billy the Kid.
Source: Library of Congress, Prints & Photographs Division,
New York World-Telegram and the Sun Newspaper Photo-
graph Collection (Library of Congress), LC-USZ62-136377

Several weeks later during the course of his flight, he arrived at Fort Sumner where he had friends and, some claimed, a girlfriend.

According to Garrett, he was visiting with Pete Maxwell in the latter's bedroom around midnight when a stranger stepped through the doorway. Wearing only socks on his feet and carrying a knife, the stranger asked, "*¿Quien es?*" (Who is it?) Believing the newcomer was Billy the Kid, the object of his search, Garrett raised his pistol and shot him through the chest, killing him.

A moment later, Garrett ran out of the room and breathlessly stated to his two deputies waiting outside, John Poe and Thomas McKinney, "Boys, that was the Kid, and I think I have got him." Poe, after leaning into the doorway and staring at the body lying on the floor, turned to Garrett and said, "Pat, the Kid would not come to this place. You have shot the wrong man."

Within minutes of the killing, residents of Fort Sumner were already whispering among themselves that the dead man was not Billy the Kid. Of the three lawmen present, evidence suggests that Poe was the only one who had never seen the Kid before. Author Leon Metz, among others, has suggested that Poe "would be inclined to accept almost any body that Garrett claimed was Billy's." Garrett could then claim the reward, says Metz, as well as the honor and prestige that went with killing the Southwest's most noted outlaw. Poe would not have known the difference. McKinney was strangely silent about the issue until many years later.

The controversy over the so-called killing of Billy the Kid was only just beginning. Not one, but three inquests followed the killing. One was made on the night of the shooting and the second the following morning. A third was to come days later. The inquests only added to the controversy. The first was "lost," and the second had all of the earmarks of having been coerced, as some have suggested, by Garrett in order to make himself look good.

It has also been implied that the second inquest was a forgery. According to at least one writer, only three of the six witnesses who signed the report had actually seen the body, and one of them later stated that it was *not* the Kid who had been shot. Neither of the first two documents was ever officially recorded, and to date there exists no legal proof of the death of Billy the Kid at the hands of Pat Garrett.

The burial of the body of the man slain by Garrett remains as controversial as the shooting and the inquest. The body that was placed in the casket was described by newspaperman S. M. Ashenfelter as having dark skin and a beard. Six and one-half months prior to the shooting, however, J. H. Koogler, the editor of New Mexico's *Las Vegas Gazette*, interviewed the young outlaw while he was in town waiting to be transferred to Mesilla for trial. At the time, Koogler described the Kid as looking like "a mere boy . . . looking like a schoolboy, with the traditional silky fuzz on his upper lip . . . light hair and complexion."

Based on the descriptions by Ashenfelter and Koogler, the body in the casket could not have belonged to Billy the Kid. According to the leading textbooks on endocrinology, along with expert advice from physicians, the biological processes associated with such rapid changes in hair growth and skin color simply do not exist. The body in the casket was not that of Billy the Kid.

The current gravesite for Billy the Kid in Fort Sumner is not even authentic. The marker is a tourist attraction, nothing more. Only very few people knew where the body of the man slain by Garrett was buried. Since the interment, floods from the nearby Pecos River have ravaged the old cemetery, sometimes transporting headstones and caskets miles downstream. On another occasion, most of the bodies were disinterred and removed without identification to the Santa Fe National Cemetery.

Following the burial, things in Lincoln County quieted down somewhat, but the residents continued to whisper among themselves about the escape of their friend, Billy the Kid. In the years that followed, the Kid was reportedly seen many times by close friends and others who knew him. He even returned to Lincoln to visit his old friend, Yginio Salazar.

Since 1881, a number of men have come forth and claimed to be the outlaw, Billy the Kid. Most were not taken seriously because they were the wrong age, had the wrong look, and were clearly imposters. Now and then, however, someone surfaced who invited closer scrutiny.

A likely candidate, at least initially, was a man who went by the name of John Miller and lived in Ramah, New Mexico. He passed away in 1933 in Arizona. A few old-time Ramah residents were convinced Miller was the famous outlaw. Two researchers, Helen Airy and Daniel Bartie, were also convinced Miller was the Kid and set out to try to prove it. A book followed, but it did little or nothing to provide evidence in support of the contention that Miller might have been the Kid. The only "evidence" offered for Miller being the famous outlaw was that he said he was.

In 1948, a paralegal working on an estate settlement in Florida accidentally learned about a man living in Texas some old-timers claimed was Billy the Kid. After driving across several states and interviewing a number of people, William V. Morrison eventually tracked down a man named William Henry Roberts in the small town of Hamilton.

On meeting Roberts, Morrison told him he possessed evidence that suggested he was Billy the Kid. Roberts denied it. Following a conversation, Morrison rose to leave when Roberts, not wanting his wife to hear him, approached and whispered an invitation to return the following day so they could talk in private.

The next morning, Roberts sent his wife on an errand after Morrison arrived and, once the two men were alone, admitted he was Billy the Kid. He said his wife was not even aware of it and that he had tried to keep the secret for many years because he believed he was still under sentence to be hanged. He wondered if there was any way he could be pardoned for his crimes.

Morrison responded like any good legal worker would: He suggested he might be able to help arrange for such a thing but needed proof of his identity. He told Roberts that he was aware of some bullet wounds suffered by the Kid and asked to see the scars. Obliging, Roberts doffed his shirt and trousers and pointed out those listed by Morrison and about twenty others.

Morrison reminded Roberts that the Kid was known to be able to slip out of a pair of handcuffs. Without hesitation, Roberts responded by holding out his hands and in a double-jointed move tucked each thumb inside his palms, thus making his hands smaller than his wrists. Morrison asked numerous questions about Billy the Kid and the Lincoln County War and Roberts had all of the correct answers in spite of the fact that he could barely read and write.

While not absolutely certain, Morrison was growing confident Roberts might be the Kid. He made arrangements for the old man to travel with him to Lincoln County, New Mexico, where he wanted to question him in detail on specific aspects of the Lincoln County War. He wanted Roberts to try to remember incidents that might have some bearing on his pardon. He also wanted to introduce Roberts to people who were still living that had known Billy the Kid.

It turned out to be an incredible journey for both men. During the ride, Roberts recalled a number of prevalent details about the conflict, about personalities involved, about places, and about the politics of those days. Roberts related details that, at the time, were unknown to the historians.

Roberts told Morrison that on the night of July 14, 1881, in Fort Sumner, it was not he who went to Pete Maxwell's bedroom, but a friend named Billy Barlow. Barlow, who was identified as being half-Mexican, was a year or two younger than Roberts and approximately the same size and general appearance. Following a dance, Roberts, Barlow, Saval Gutierrez, and a woman stopped at the dwelling of Jesus Silva. As Silva prepared a meal for his visitors, he discovered he was out of meat and told his guests there was a freshly cut beef hanging near Maxwell's room. Barlow, in his stockinged feet and carrying only a knife, went to retrieve some. It was Barlow, said Roberts, whom Garrett mistook for Billy the Kid.

When Roberts heard the shooting, he grabbed his pistols and headed toward the Maxwell dwelling. He was fired upon by Garrett and the deputies and struck in the lower jaw, in the back near the left shoulder, and suffered a grazing wound across the top of his head. Dazed and bleeding, Roberts stumbled into a nearby house where an old Mexican woman hid him and tended to his wounds.

The next morning at 3:00 AM, a friend brought Billy the Kid's horse to the woman's abode and told him that Garrett killed Barlow and was passing the body off as that of the outlaw. Roberts was soon joined by another friend, Frank Lobato, and after thanking the old woman, the two men mounted up and rode off into the darkness.

Billy the Kid was anxious to put some distance between himself and the law. Since he was under a death sentence, he feared he might be found and returned to Lincoln County to hang. He decided to flee to Mexico.

During the next several decades, Roberts, who went by a number of aliases, said he worked on ranches in Mexico and the United States, served in Teddy Roosevelt's Rough Riders in Cuba, joined the army of Pancho Villa during the Mexican Revolution, worked for Wild West shows, broke horses, and even had a varied career in law enforcement. When Morrison met him he was going by the alias Ollie L. Roberts, the name of a deceased relative. He married three times but never had any children of his own. He was eighty-eight years old when Morrison found him in Hamilton, Texas.

On November 15, 1950, Morrison petitioned for a pardon for William Henry Roberts, aka Billy the Kid, with then New Mexico governor Thomas J. Mabry. Mabry agreed to meet with Roberts and Morrison on November 30. Despite assurances that the meeting would be private, Mabry, ever the politician, went back on his word and announced it to the media and invited the press to attend along with relatives of Pat Garrett and other descendants of Lincoln County War figures.

The meeting was a farce, with Mabry and others asking Roberts questions that had nothing to do whatsoever with his petition or with seeking the truth. The petition was never considered by the governor and the pardon was denied. Dejected, Roberts returned to his home, now in Hico, Texas. Two months later he collapsed on a Hico sidewalk. Moments later, he was dead from a heart attack.

Could William Henry Roberts have been Billy the Kid? In 1955, Harvard-educated Dr. C. L. Sonnichsen, with help from Morrison, released the book *Alias Billy the Kid* that detailed aspects of Roberts's life as the famous outlaw. In the book, Roberts was described as an illiterate man who could barely read and write but was keenly intimate with events and people associated with the Lincoln County War. There can be no doubt that he participated in the conflict. While the Sonnichsen-Morrison case for Roberts being the Kid was fascinating and compelling, it left numerous gaps and failed to convince many who clung to the historical status quo. While Sonnichsen had few peers as a writer, researcher, and chronicler of things Southwestern, neither he nor Morrison were experts on Lincoln County War history, and they didn't ask Roberts enough of the right questions. It was clear that the uneducated Roberts knew more about the war and its participants than anyone, and he spoke with the conviction of someone who was there when it was happening. In the end, Sonnichsen wondered in print, "If Roberts was not the Kid, then who was he?"

Indeed, who was William Henry Roberts? Since the publication of *Alias Billy the Kid*, there have been dozens of attempts to disprove Roberts was the Kid. Many of these attempts emanated from the state of New Mexico, which is the beneficiary of what they claim is a multimillion-dollar tourist industry built around the famous outlaw. The majority of the attempts to discredit Roberts were the result of poor research design and advanced by many who had no credentials whatsoever. It has been suggested that some of these attempts were politically motivated. The responses to the notion that Roberts could be the Kid offered nothing new, and only repeated the already suspect and discredited history concerning the matter.

One of the most widely publicized attempts to dismiss Roberts as the Kid was undertaken in 1988 by an organization called the Lincoln County Heritage Trust (LCHT) under the leadership of a man named Robert L. Hart. The trust approved a photo-comparison project designed to examine real and alleged images of Billy the Kid. According to Hart, Roberts "was to become the prime focus of attention with the immediate goal of . . . publicity" for the LCHT. In the end, using a computer technique designed by Thomas G. Kyle, Roberts was rejected as being the Kid. For reasons known only to Kyle and other members of the project, the only statistically reliable photo-comparison technique available in the world at the time, one that had been around for seventeen years, was ignored. Instead, Kyle employed a self-created technique that provided for no statistical validity whatsoever.

A few serious Billy the Kid scholars were appalled by the LCHT project. It was amateurish, not worthy of support from a professional organization, not worth the thousands of dollars paid for it, and was clearly designed to support a previously determined decision. The design and undertaking of the LCHT analysis was deemed unprofessional and a "complete distortion" by professionals, and one that proved embarrassing to the LCHT.

Based on a subsequent magazine article penned by Kyle, it became clear he knew nothing about photo-comparison and identification analysis technique and procedure. Despite the unsophisticated nature of this photo-comparison project, all of the so-called Billy the Kid and Lincoln County War experts associated with it went against elementary investigative and research procedure, as well as logic and common sense, by accepting and endorsing the results without question.

A legitimate photo-comparison study, however, was not long in coming. The stunning results, coupled with the findings of one of the few professional investigations undertaken on the Kid, were reported in *Billy the Kid: Beyond the Grave* (2005).

Summarizing a total of forty-plus years of research and study, the book provides critical analysis of most of the Billy the Kid scholarship of the past one hundred years and presented thus far the clearest and most compelling evidence that the famous outlaw was not killed by Pat Garrett but lived for another sixty-nine years.

Following an intensive examination of the existing history of Billy the Kid, particularly the so-called killing by Garrett, much of it was discovered to be flawed, in error, and contradictory. Ultimately it was determined that what most people think they know about the killing of Billy the Kid, including some of the subject's most prominent researchers, for the most part comes from only one person—Pat Garrett. History is replete with examples of Garrett's lack of veracity, thus anything attributed to him is suspect. In later years he was dismissed from his job as Collector of Customs for lying to President Theodore

Roosevelt. Garrett's version of events related to the shooting, as well as many other observations on Billy the Kid found in his book, *The Authentic Life of Billy the Kid*, was actually written by someone else, an alcoholic entrepreneur named Ashmon Upson. Critics have not been kind to Garrett since *Authentic Life* was originally published in 1882. Dozens of errors and outright lies have been discovered in the text. Yet, to a large extent this publication is considered by many to be the authoritative reference on the life and death of Billy the Kid.

In addition to pointing out the flaws associated with the "accepted" history of the outlaw, *Billy the Kid: Beyond the Grave* provides a genealogy of William Henry Roberts, one that was found in an old family Bible belonging to relatives. The genealogy solves a number of problems long encountered by historians. Among other things, it shows that Roberts was related to people named Antrim, McCarty, and Bonney, names he used as aliases.

Billy the Kid: Beyond the Grave also provides the results of investigations into elements of Roberts's descriptions of what became of his life following his escape from Fort Sumner. Roberts's versions of events were tracked down in order to make a determination relative to his veracity. Where materials and documents could be found, they verified Roberts's version of events. Ultimately, Roberts's credibility far exceeded that of Pat Garrett.

Tapes of interviews with Roberts conducted by Morrison were provided by his descendants, and the words of the man who would be Billy the Kid were listened to and transcribed, words that provided incredible detail and insight relative to people, places, and things associated with the Lincoln County War, words that could only have come from someone who was there when it was happening, words that revealed a knowledge and intimacy of the Lincoln County War and related events that far exceeded that of the so-called experts of the day.

In perhaps the most startling Billy the Kid revelation of modern times, a legitimate photo-comparison evaluation of Roberts and the outlaw was conducted. The technique was the only recognized and statistically valid one in use in the world at the time, and was used by the FBI, CIA, Interpol, Scotland Yard, and other major law enforcement agencies. It compared facial features and facial relationships between the only authenticated image of Billy the Kid and a photograph of Roberts taken when he was eighty-eight years old.

Using state-of-the-art facilities at the University of Texas at Austin Vision Systems and Advanced Graphics Laboratory, the images were digitized and image-improved employing a variety of techniques. Images were scanned and digitized into an image 512 by 512 bytes, computing an LoG (Laplacian of a Gaussian) edge map, identifying reference points, determining feature distances, and computing an error estimate for the match. Features measured included interpupillary distance, internal biocular breadth, external biocular breadth, nose breadth, mouth breadth, bizygomatic breadth (cheekbones), mid-lip to chin distance, mid-lip to nose distance, and nose length.

Compared to the Billy the Kid tintype, Roberts's measurements showed a remarkable likeness and yielded a mean standard error of only 17.7. According to the analysts, "the similarity between the facial structure of . . . Roberts and the man in the . . . tintype is amazing." Only minor discrepancies existed, and they were explained away by differences in weight and the fact that Roberts, at eighty-eight years of age, had no teeth.

In and of itself, this high-tech photo-comparison study proves a remarkable similarity. Placed side by side with other compelling evidence presented in *Beyond the Grave*, including the genealogy, Roberts's own testimony, and the testimony of others, it presents a formidable case for the notion that Pat Garrett did not kill the Kid.

Some who continued to maintain the position that the Kid died at the hands of Garrett attempted to dispute the findings presented in *Billy the Kid: Beyond the Grave*, but never provided anything in the way of substantive criticism or enlightenment.

Given the evidence, the so-called shooting of Billy the Kid by Pat Garrett may remain less of a mystery than those associated with Garrett's own motives and his ultimate death. Many questions have been posed on these topics, but few have been adequately answered.

Did Pat Garrett know he did not kill Billy the Kid? Many believe this was the case and ask why he would pass the body off as that of the famous outlaw knowing there was the possibility that the Kid might return. Perhaps Metz's speculation was correct when he suggested that the sheriff did so for the reward as well as the honor and prestige. One must also remember that Garrett was a politician, and it is possible that he saw the attendant publicity for killing the most wanted man in the Southwest as a springboard to the future electability and higher office for which he longed. Perhaps Garrett was convinced that, once escaped and presumed safe, the Kid would never return to tell a different story. Perhaps, as some believe, Garrett and the Kid concocted a scheme wherein the outlaw was allowed to escape. These mysteries, along with those associated with Garrett's own death, may never be solved.

Why did deputies Poe and McKinney support Garrett's contention that it was Billy the Kid who was gunned down in Maxwell's bedroom? The truth is, statements and testimony later attributed to Garrett, Poe, and McKinney are contradictory. It was Poe who initially informed Garrett that he killed the wrong man. While outwardly loyal and supportive of the sheriff, Poe, in his book *The Death of Billy the Kid* published in 1933, referred to the circumstances of the shooting as a "mystery."

The idea has been advanced, and evidence provided that Poe and McKinney went along with Garrett's version of the shooting because they were Masonic Lodge brothers. During McKinney's later years, according to a cousin, he admitted that the Kid got away and that the truth of the shooting at Fort Sumner was not as it was related by Garrett.

Unlike Billy the Kid, when Garrett was shot and killed there was no question of who the victim was. Garrett for certain, would never return.

Billy the Kid, on the other hand, most certainly did.

TWO

◆◆◆

Who Killed Pat Garrett?

During the fifty-three years of his life, Patrick Floyd Jarvis Garrett was many things: buffalo hunter, cowhand, lawman, Texas Ranger, rancher, customs collector, gambler, philanderer, and more. All of his occupations and activities, however, have been overshadowed by the notion that Garrett, as sheriff of New Mexico's Lincoln County, shot and killed the notorious outlaw Billy the Kid. Whether or not Garrett actually killed the Kid has been debated, sometimes hotly, during the past century, and accumulating evidence keeps Garrett's contention open to question. Whatever the case, there is little doubt that the bulk of Garrett's fame hinges on that single event.

Surrounded by mystery during most of his life, Garrett's death has also proven baffling. That the former sheriff was shot and killed in the desert a few miles from Las Cruces has never been open to question. To this day, however, there is little consensus on who actually murdered the former sheriff, and as many as five likely suspects have been identified.

Born in Chambers County, Alabama, on June 5, 1850, Garrett moved with his family to Louisiana when he was quite young. When the elder Garrett died, Pat, not inclined to become involved in disagreements with his siblings over how property should be divided, simply mounted a horse and rode away to Texas.

On arriving in the High Plains region of Texas, Garrett occasionally found work as a cowhand and buffalo hunter during the 1870s. While in camp during one hunting season, Garrett killed his first man, a fellow hunter named Joe Brisco. The killing was judged to be self-defense, and Garrett was never formally charged. During the late 1870s, Garrett moved to Fort Sumner, New Mexico, and went to work as a cowhand for landowner and rancher Pete Maxwell.

Following the conflict that has been called the Lincoln County War, Garrett ran for the office of sheriff of Lincoln County. One of his campaign promises was to rid the region of the outlaw Billy the Kid. Garrett won the election, and a short time later he had the Kid under lock and key in the Lincoln County Jail. Captured at Stinking Springs, the Kid was subsequently tried in Las Cruces, found guilty of killing Sheriff William Brady, and sentenced to hang on April 28, 1881, in Lincoln where he was delivered to await execution.

To Garrett's embarrassment, Billy the Kid escaped from the jail, killing two lawmen in the process—William Bell and Robert Olinger. The sheriff, with help from other lawmen, eventually trailed the Kid to Fort Sumner. In his own words, Garrett claimed he shot the Kid from the darkness of Pete Maxwell's bedroom when the outlaw stepped into it after spotting deputies John Poe and Thomas McKinney outside. The events of that evening, as well as the person killed by Garrett, have long been disputed.

Following that night, Garrett's luck began to change for the worse. His claim for the reward for killing Billy the Kid was denied. His political career, which had bright prospects up to that point, began unraveling. He lost his bid for reelection to sheriff and drifted into work as a cattle buyer and land speculator. Bad weather and other factors eventually forced him to look elsewhere for employment.

Garrett, along with an alcoholic postman cum journalist named Ashmon Upson, became involved in writing a book titled *The Authentic Life of Billy the Kid, the Noted Desperado of the Southwest, Whose Deeds of Daring Have Made His Name a Terror in New Mexico, Arizona, and Northern Mexico.* Upson did most of the writing, with Garrett contributing little more than his name and a few vignettes. The result was a ludicrous tome filled with fanciful tales and made-up events pertaining to the life and times of the outlaw. Though no serious Western scholar considers the book truthful, it unfortunately remains the basis for most of what many people believe about the Kid. The book was a financial failure for Garrett and Upson.

In 1887, Garrett began promoting the notion of damming the Rio Hondo to provide irrigation water for the desert near Roswell, New Mexico. He involved wealthy and prominent cattlemen and bankers and eventually formed the Pecos Valley Land and Ditch Company. As a result of financial problems, however, the company was restructured. In the process, Garrett's role was eliminated. A short time later he moved to Uvalde, Texas.

When noted attorney and statesman Colonel Albert Jennings Fountain and his nine-year-old son Henry mysteriously disappeared in New Mexico in 1896, Garrett was summoned by Governor William T. Thornton to investigate the case. Garrett suspected the pair was murdered by Jim Gilliland, Oliver Lee, and Bill McNew—all cowmen who were politically connected with Albert Bacon Fall, a staunch Fountain enemy.

After assembling a posse, Garrett tracked the suspects to a cabin at Wildy Well, forty-five miles east of Las Cruces. Unknown to the lawmen, the suspects were sleeping on the roof of the structure when Garrett banged into the cabin and leveled his revolver at one of the occupants—a woman. One of the posse members grew suspicious and decided to check the roof. He was shot for his effort. Taken completely by surprise, Garrett and the posse men were forced to surrender, relinquish their guns, and ride away. Word of Garrett's humiliating debacle soon spread throughout the region, causing further embarrassment for the former lawman.

Gilliland, Lee, and McNew eventually turned themselves in and, with Fall as their lawyer, went to trial. In a very short time the three men were acquitted, and the disappearance of Albert Jennings Fountain remains one of the most puzzling mysteries of the American West (see chapter 3, "The Mysterious Disappearance of Colonel Albert Jennings Fountain").

In 1901, Garrett was appointed collector of customs by President Theodore Roosevelt, a position he managed to bungle. After four years, Roosevelt declined to reappoint Garrett after the former sheriff was caught lying to the president. By 1906, Garrett and his family had returned to his ranch in Dona Ana County. Poor management of his resources, along with continued gambling and whoring, eventually led to Garrett getting deeper in debt, mortgaged to the hilt, and in need of money.

In 1907, James P. Miller offered Garrett $3,000 for his ranch. Miller was a curious character with a deadly reputation and proved to be a rather dangerous neighbor. A known assassin, Killin' Jim Miller is believed to have been responsible for the deaths of at least thirty men.

Miller told Garrett he wanted the ranch as a location to hold cattle from Mexico until they were sold, but evidence suggests he probably wanted the property to hide illegal Chinese immigrants he was smuggling from south of the border. Perhaps seeing a way he could pay off some of his growing debts and make a little money in the bargain,

Garrett agreed to sell. Unfortunately, prior to the sale Garrett's son, Poe, agreed to lease the land to Wayne Brazel to raise goats on. To speed up the sale, Miller decided to purchase Brazel's goats. Brazel told Miller his herd numbered 1,200. Miller offered $3.50 a head, an offer that was accepted. Several days later, however, Brazel returned to Miller and told him that he miscounted, that he had 1,800 goats.

Miller insisted on staying with the original deal, and that angered Brazel. With tempers flaring, Garrett agreed to help settle the matter. Garrett, Brazel, and Miller's representative Carl Adamson agreed to meet in Las Cruces to negotiate a settlement.

Adamson picked Garrett up on his ranch on February 29, 1908, and followed a road through the Organ Mountains toward Las Cruces. After coming through a pass and descending the west side of the range, the pair overtook Brazel who was on horseback and riding ahead of them. Some historians claim Brazel was seen in the company of another horseman who, on spotting the oncoming wagon carrying Garrett and Adamson, rode away into the desert.

Almost from the moment they met that day, Garrett and Brazel argued heatedly about the goats. When the men were five miles from Las Cruces, Adamson halted the wagon and called for a break. Garrett stepped down from the wagon, removed his left glove, turned his back to the two men, and began urinating. A moment later a bullet struck him in the back of the head, likely killing him instantly.

Wayne Brazel confessed to the murder, claiming self-defense. He was arrested and held for a trial that was scheduled for October. The trial was a sham, incompetently prosecuted and defended. Very few witnesses for either side were called. Prosecuting Attorney Mark B. Thompson, as it turned out, was a close friend and political ally of Brazel's defense attorneys. Following a short trial and an even shorter jury deliberation, Brazel was found not guilty.

In spite of the trial, and in spite of what appears to many on the surface to be a cut-and-dried determination regarding the killer of Pat Garrett, very few people at the time believed Brazel was guilty or that he was even capable of such an act. Regardless of the outcome, the actual murderer of Pat Garrett remains a mystery to this day.

While Wayne Brazel certainly cannot be eliminated from suspicion as the killer of Garrett, there exist several confusing elements, most notably Brazel's plea of self-defense. Garrett was facing away from his slayer while urinating, hardly a threatening posture. Furthermore, once he was down on the ground and presumably dead, Garrett was shot once again, this time in the stomach.

The physician who examined Garrett's body stated that the first bullet entered the back of the head "just below the hat line and exited at the right eyebrow." Regarding the killing shot, Garrett biographer and apologist Leon Metz wrote, "Only a person on horseback, or shooting from a higher elevation, could have fired it." Experienced crime scene investigators disagree with Metz's analysis because it fails to take into consideration a number of elements. The term "hat line" is undefined and meaningless, since it can vary depending on how one wears one's hat. Additionally, Metz's observation does not take into consideration the simple possibility that Garrett's head could have been tilted in a variety of directions as he looked at the horizon, the ground, his boots, or a cactus as he was urinating. Simple logic and common sense eliminate the assumption that only a person on horseback could have fired the weapon that sent a bullet though Garrett's head.

Furthermore, the medical evidence available suggests that Garrett was shot by two different bullets, only one of which may have come from Brazel's Colt .45. Author Chuck Hornung has written that "Brazel . . . might have dismounted and placed the second shot into Garrett's body as a show of support for his partner, Print Rhode, who may have fired the first shot from ambush."

Despite the outcome of the trial, Wayne Brazel's role in the killing of Garrett remains obscure. Several researchers have suggested that Brazel was a bit simple-minded, easily duped, and may have been persuaded to take the blame for the killing with the promise that he would eventually be found innocent.

The only investigation ever conducted of the Garrett murder was done by Fred Fornoff who, at the time of the killing, was the director of the New Mexico Mounted Police. Fornoff was convinced there was a conspiracy among several men to kill Garrett, and he was personally convinced that Brazel did not pull the trigger. Unfortunately, Fornoff's records have been destroyed.

The aforementioned Print Rhode has often been promoted as a suspect. Rhode was, in fact, partnered with Brazel in the goat business. It was also a fact that Rhode and Garrett had argued on several occasions.

Another suspect in the Garrett killing was Carl Adamson, the driver of the wagon. Members of Garrett's family suspected Adamson from the beginning. Officially, he was the only other person present, and he certainly had the opportunity. The problem with Adamson as a suspect is that he does not appear to have an obvious motive. If not the actual killer, many suggest, Adamson was likely part of the plot.

William Webb Cox has also been advanced as a possible suspect. While it is fairly certain that Cox did not shoot Garrett, it has been suggested that he might have paid to have the job done. It has been speculated that Cox wanted the Garrett Ranch, and that the only way for him to get it was to have Garrett killed. It has been further speculated that Cox hired noted assassin Killin' Jim Miller to do the job and perhaps convinced Wayne Brazel to take the blame, assuring him he would be taken care of.

Some suspect that Adamson may have been involved in a conspiracy along with Brazel, their roles being associated with setting Garrett up so that Miller could kill him. Following Brazel's acquittal, Cox threw a celebration party at his own ranch, featuring the goat rancher as the guest of honor. There exists, however, no indisputable evidence to support Cox's role as an organizer and conspirator.

New Mexico lawman Dee Harkey was convinced Garrett was killed by Miller. Harkey claims Miller stopped by his ranch in Roosevelt County and asked to borrow a horse from one of his cowhands, a man named Joe Beasley. According to Beasley, Miller then rode the horse to Otero County and back the following day, a considerable distance. Though Beasley had no reason to lie about this incident, he did possess the reputation of being a less than honest man.

Harkey himself noticed the poor condition of the horse and asked Beasley about it. Beasley replied, "Miller rode him over and killed Pat Garrett and told me what he had done. He said that if he was ever indicted for it, he was going to expect to show by me that he was here at your ranch at the time Garrett was killed."

According to Harkey, Miller bragged to at least one other person that he had killed Pat Garrett. Killin' Jim Miller was never arrested for the crime or even officially considered a suspect.

Lawman Fornoff, on investigating the site where the killing took place, found tracks of a shod horse, a spent rifle shell, and several cigarette butts on a sand hill about fifty feet away, suggesting someone may have waited in ambush. This pattern was consistent with Miller's method of assassination.

Fornoff also interrogated Wayne Brazel and was persuaded that the simple man was innocent of the shooting. Brazel's responses to questions were often contradictory and Fornoff maintained the confessed killer's account of what happened made no sense whatsoever. Furthermore, people who knew Brazel were convinced he could not have killed anyone.

Ultimately, Fornoff developed the theory that W. W. Cox was ultimately responsible for the killing of Garrett, and that Print Rhode and rancher Oliver Lee were involved in the plot. Each of these men, all known cattle rustlers, hated Garrett, and each had been arrested at least once by the lawman. While it was never clear that Fornoff believed Jim Miller actually pulled the trigger, the lawman was convinced the well-known killer was in league with Cox. Fornoff was also convinced that Carl Adamson was the man who fired the second round into Garrett's stomach.

Over a century has passed since the killing of Pat Garrett, one of the American West's most interesting and complicated lawmen. In spite of ongoing research and investigative efforts, no one is any closer to determining the identity of his murderer today than they were in 1907.

THREE

The Mysterious Disappearance of
Colonel Albert Jennings Fountain

When Colonel Albert Jennings Fountain and his young son Henry climbed onto the buckboard on that cold January day in 1896, they had no notion that within seventy-two hours they would become two of the principal characters in one of the greatest mysteries in all of the American West. Both Fountain and his son disappeared and were presumed killed. To this day, however, no one knows for certain what happened to them, whether or not they were murdered, and if so, who committed the acts. The bodies of Fountain and his son have never been found.

Albert J. Fountain was an important figure in American history. He was a member of the original California Column that marched from the Golden State to New Mexico during the Civil War. After serving his term in the army, Fountain organized a civilian militia to protect New Mexican settlers from raiding Apache and Navajo Indians. In addition, Fountain often led militia raids against outlaws and any others who would terrorize the state's citizens.

During one battle with Navajos during which he fought bravely, Fountain was seriously wounded. While recuperating in an El Paso hospital, Fountain developed an interest in politics. As he nurtured his growing political ambitions, Fountain founded a newspaper in Mesilla, New Mexico, wherein he dealt primarily with governmental issues. His frank and often-critical editorials angered many.

Fountain was also Billy the Kid's defense attorney during the outlaw's trial at Mesilla. Here, Fountain did not fare well, for the Kid was found guilty and sentenced to hang.

In 1888 Fountain, a Republican, won a bid for the New Mexico legislature, badly beating his opponent, an aggressive politician and

staunch Democrat named Albert Bacon Fall. While serving at the state
capitol of Santa Fe, the well-respected Fountain was elected Speaker
of the House. In the 1892 election, Fountain was defeated by Fall
following a hotly contested campaign. Each man harbored an intense
and deepening dislike for the other.

At the time of his mysterious disappearance, Fountain was serving
as special prosecutor for the Southeastern New Mexico Livestock Association and had only days earlier secured grand jury indictments
against thirty-two men for cattle theft. Among those indicted were a
number of prominent area ranchers including Jim Gilliland, Oliver
Lee, and William McNew. McNew was a good friend of and sometime
business partner with Albert Bacon Fall. The rift growing between
Fountain and Fall became well known throughout the region, and
some historians are convinced Fountain's indictments were simply a
way to create problems for his political enemy.

Word leaked out that Fountain was working on the indictments, and
the special prosecutor subsequently received numerous threats on his
life. On the very morning he readied himself and Henry for a long trip
to his home in Mesilla, some one hundred miles to the southwest as
the crow flies, he was handed a note that contained the threat that he
would be killed within the week if he did not drop the rustling charges.

Fountain treated the note as he had all of the other threats—he simply
ignored it and refused to allow it to cause him to change his plans. After
wrapping Henry warmly in a blanket and quilt in the buckboard seat
next to him, he snapped the reins across the back of his team of horses,
one white and one black, and set off down the road that led to Mesilla
and home. It is believed by many that Fountain took Henry with him
on business trips as a result of the urging of his wife, Mariana, who was
convinced no one would harm the prosecutor accompanied by a nine-
year-old child. Mariana would soon regret her decision.

The first day of travel was leisurely and uneventful, and the Fountains spent the night at Blazer's Mill, located on the west side of the
Mescalero Apache Indian Reservation. On the following morning, a
Friday, Colonel Fountain and Henry got an early start and were on
the road shortly after dawn. They had not traveled far when they
encountered a Mescalero Apache who stopped them. The Indian was
leading a pinto pony. The Apache owed a debt to Fountain and offered the horse as payment. The two men spoke briefly, and Fountain
finally accepted the pony, tied it to the rear of the buckboard, and set
off down the road once again.

Around noon the Fountains arrived at the town of Tularosa, and the colonel pulled the buckboard to a stop in front of a mercantile operated by his friend Albert Dieter. Dieter offered to provide lunch for the Fountains but the colonel declined, requesting only a quantity of oats for his team of horses. After leaving Tularosa, Fountain and his son rode for a few more hours along the well-traveled route before finally stopping at the La Luz settlement where they spent the night with a resident named Sutherland.

The next morning after stowing gear, his satchel, and Winchester repeating rifle into the buckboard, Fountain tucked Henry into the seat and set off. He was not looking forward to this leg of the journey, for he faced a long and arduous ride across the arid basin that lay between La Luz and Las Cruces. Earlier, Fountain had made arrangements to transport Miss Fannie Stevenson to Las Cruces that day, but because the weather was so bitingly cold, she declined to go.

As he pulled out of La Luz, Fountain reined up for a few minutes to visit with a man named Hill who was riding into town. Hill later recalled that Fountain mentioned he had seen three men on horseback riding along the trail ahead of him.

Around lunchtime, Fountain halted the buckboard at a location called Pellman's Well near what is now White Sands National Monument. Fountain gave the horses a break, fed and watered them, and had a quiet and restful lunch with Henry.

About two hours later on the road, Fountain met mail carrier Santos Alvarado. Alvarado had completed a delivery to Luna's Well and was on his way back to Tularosa. After the two visited for a few minutes, Fountain asked Alvarado if he had seen three riders on the road up ahead. The mailman acknowledged that he had, but stated that they turned off the main road and traveled eastward in the direction of the Sacramento Mountains. The two men spoke briefly of other things and Fountain continued on.

A little farther down the road, Fountain encountered a group of five riders traveling toward Tularosa. Among them was another mail carrier and old friend Saturnino Barela. During a brief conversation, Fountain mentioned the three men he had seen some distance up ahead. Barela told Fountain his party had apparently encountered the same three men on the trail some distance back, but when the strangers spotted the travelers they quickly left the trail and rode away. Concerned that the strangers might represent a potential threat to the colonel, Barela advised Fountain to return to Luna's Well and remain for the night. In the morning, promised Barela, he would accompany them on their journey as far as Las Cruces.

Fountain thanked Barela for his offer and told him he was determined to reach home before midnight. With a wave to his friend, the colonel continued down the road. Saturnino Barela may have been the last man to see Albert Jennings Fountain and his son Henry alive. The last, that is, except for the killers.

The next morning, February 2, Barela was on his way to Mesilla down the same road he had traveled the previous day. About three miles beyond the point where he had visited with Fountain, Barela was cresting the low ridge of Chalk Hill when he spotted some unusual signs of disturbance along the trail. It was apparent to Barela that something terrible had occurred there, and he rushed on to Mesilla.

On arriving in town, Barela contacted Fountain's son, Albert, Jr., and explained what he saw. The younger Fountain, already concerned over the whereabouts of his father and brother, hastily assembled a group of friends to ride out to Chalk Hill to investigate. Due to the dark night and extreme cold, the group of men had little luck in determining anything.

The next morning they were joined by another posse that included some experienced trackers. After studying the area thoroughly, they found tracks of three horses, some spent cartridges, and a place where Fountain's wagon was either driven or led off the main road toward the south. A short distance away, the buckboard had apparently stopped and then continued on. On the ground near the wagon tracks at this site, the desert sand was splotched with a great deal of blood. The men in the search party concluded that the Fountains were ambushed at Chalk Hill, led off the main road, and then killed at this spot.

Later that afternoon the posse found Fountain's buckboard sitting abandoned about a dozen miles south of Chalk Hill. Blood, now dried, was splattered across the vehicle. Lying on the floor of the wagon were Henry's hat, Fountain's tie, and a number of other possessions that were apparently removed from the prosecutor's satchel, inspected, and tossed away.

Tracks clearly showed that three riders accompanied the buckboard to this point, unhitched the team of horses, and rode away toward the east. The pinto pony tied to the back of the buckboard had either broken loose or been cut away. Its tracks led northward.

Following the tracks of the three riders and two extra horses, the posse traveled another five miles where they found a poor camp among some low bushes. Here, the quarry had cooked a fast meal over a fire and fed the mounts. One of Fountain's horses, the white one, apparently broke away from the camp and ran off into the desert. A small group of trackers followed this horse while the others continued along the trail of the three riders and the black horse. Later in the day the white horse was found at St. Nicolas Spring, the hair on its back coated with blood as if a dead or seriously wounded person had ridden it or been tied to it.

Three miles from the camp the tracks diverged. Two riders, leading Fountain's horse rode through the northernmost pass through the Jarilla Mountains. Their trail led to the Dog Canyon Ranch that was owned by Oliver Lee. The remaining rider turned southeast and rode through an adjacent pass located immediately south of the first. The trackers separated into two groups, one following the two riders and the other following the lone rider. When the party following the two riders was within three miles of Lee's ranch they found that the tracks had been obliterated by a passing herd of cattle.

The other group tracking the lone rider followed a clear trail to Wildy Well, also part of Lee's huge ranching empire. In addition to a freshwater well, a couple of low stone buildings occupied the site. Here, the posse found Lee and a few of his men working. After explaining what they were looking for, Lee allowed the posse members to water their horses and then sent them on their way.

The search for the Fountains continued until Wednesday when the trackers ran out of provisions and were forced to return to Mesilla. During the following weeks, other search parties scoured the desert for Colonel Fountain and Henry but found no trace of either.

Interest in the fate of the Fountains picked up momentum during the next few weeks, and news of the disappearance reached far and wide. Those working hard for New Mexico statehood at the time feared the image of a wild and woolly frontier containing a significant outlaw element might destroy its chances. Authorities decided something must be done, so in a public relations-style move, they invited former lawman Pat Garrett to investigate the whereabouts of Colonel Fountain.

At the time, Garrett had been out of law enforcement for many years and was living in Uvalde, Texas. State officials believed his high profile and reputation as the lawman who claimed to have gunned down the outlaw Billy the Kid was certain to generate positive newspaper headlines and convince everyone that the state of New Mexico was serious about bringing criminals to justice.

Garrett was joined by Pinkerton detective agents. Working with Judge Frank Parker he obtained warrants for Bill Carr, Jim Gilliland, Oliver Lee, and William McNew. Based on the evidence, Garrett expressed confidence that these four men could be prosecuted for the kidnapping and murder of Colonel Fountain and his son.

Carr and McNew were arrested within hours. Carr was soon released for lack of evidence. Gilliland and Lee proved more difficult to locate.

Three months after the arrest of Carr and McNew, Garrett received information that the other two suspects were living and hiding at Wildy Well. Accompanied by four deputies, Garrett rode to the location, little knowing that the suspects were expecting him.

As they searched one of the buildings, the lawmen discovered Gilliland and Lee were hiding on the roof. The two fugitives opened fire from the protection of the roof's parapet, and a fierce gun battle between the officers and suspects took place over the next few seconds.

By the time the shooting was over one of the deputies was seriously wounded. Garrett and the remaining lawmen were forced to surrender and relinquish their guns. They were then ordered by Lee to leave the premises. The embarrassed lawmen rode away, leaving the wounded deputy behind. He died two days later.

Gilliland and Lee, who knew this mountain and desert region as well as anyone, remained elusive. Sometimes they hid in the mountains, sometimes at the ranches and homes of friends and sympathizers. Eventually, however, they tired of the pursuit and indicated they would surrender, but not to Garrett. They stated they would give themselves up only to Sheriff George Curry of Otero County. Curry had long been a good friend of Oliver Lee.

Otero County, formed only weeks earlier, encompassed the region where the alleged crime was presumed to have taken place. Before turning himself in to Sheriff Curry, Lee told several acquaintances that if he surrendered to Garrett, the lawman would shoot him in the back at the first opportunity. Lee and Garrett had experienced previous difficulties, and the two men did not like one another. Lee and Gilliland traveled to Las Cruces and appeared before Judge Parker. Parker ordered Sheriff Curry to escort the two men to the jail in Socorro County where they were to await trial.

Because Otero County had not yet constructed a courthouse, the trial was scheduled for Hillsboro, the seat of Sierra County. At the time, Hillsboro was a small mining town with only one hotel that had very few rooms. The town was ill prepared to accommodate the defendants, prosecutors, and witnesses, all of whom totaled close to one hundred. Trial participants were forced to live in tents that were set up at opposite ends of town, the prosecution at one end, and the defense at the other.

The prosecution was represented by Silver City District Attorney R. R. Barnes and attorneys Thomas B. Catron of Santa Fe and W. B. Childers of Albuquerque. The defendants were aided by attorneys H. M. Daugherty and Harvey Ferguson of Albuquerque and Albert B. Fall of Las Cruces. Fall was Fountain's old enemy and an increasingly powerful figure in New Mexico politics.

For strategic reasons, the prosecution withdrew the charge against McNew, but the strategy ultimately backfired. The charges pertaining to the murder of Colonel Fountain against Gilliland and Lee were also dropped. The prosecution decided their best chance was to prosecute the two men for the murder of Henry Fountain.

From the beginning the prosecution encountered difficulties. Before the trial, one of their principal witnesses, Jack Maxwell, told lawyers Barnes and Catron that he had observed Gilliland, Lee, and McNew arriving at Lee's Dog Canyon ranch only hours after the Fountains had disappeared. It was clear from the condition of the horses, according to Maxwell, that the three men had ridden hard over a long distance.

On May 29, 1899, the day the witnesses were scheduled to testify, Maxwell was nowhere to be found. He was eventually located in Alamogordo and escorted to the courthouse at Hillsboro by an Otero County deputy. After being sworn in, however, Maxwell backed off from his original testimony and offered the prosecutors very little on which to hang a case.

The principal argument for the defense, and a rather effective one, was the fact that there were no bodies, and until they could be located no one could be absolutely certain that a murder had ever been committed. After eighteen days of testimony, arguments, and counterarguments, the jury returned a verdict of not guilty.

During and after the trial, the family of Albert J. Fountain was entirely convinced that Gilliland, Lee, and McNew, perhaps in league with others, conspired to kill the prosecutor. They further believed that Henry was slain simply because he happened to be along. Even today, Fountain descendants hold firm in their belief that these three men were the murderers.

During the years following the release of Gilliland, Lee, and McNew, other suspects in the Fountain disappearance have come to the attention of researchers. According to author C. L. Sonnichsen, compelling evidence was discovered that suggested noted outlaw and train robber Black Jack Ketchum might have actually killed the colonel and his son. Quoting from an article that appeared in the May 25, 1949, issue of the *El Paso Times*, Sonnichsen related in his book *Tularosa* that Sam Ketchum told former lawman Bob Lewis that his brother, Black Jack, "murdered Colonel Fountain and his son." Sam admitted to Lewis that he was an eyewitness to the killings. Some have speculated that if Gilliland, Lee, and McNew did not kill the Fountains, they may very well have hired Ketchum to do it.

Otero County Sheriff Curry was convinced the murders were committed by Jose Chavez y Chavez, a Lincoln County War participant and friend of Billy the Kid. Following the Lincoln County War, Fountain worked hard to get Chavez y Chavez sentenced to a long term in prison. The Mexican came away from the experience with a deep and abiding hatred for the colonel, one he nursed for years. According to Curry, Chavez y Chavez once told him, "I will get that scoundrel, Fountain, if I have to hang for it." Furthermore, according to Curry, Chavez y Chavez was at Luna's Well on the evening prior to Fountain's disappearance.

Albert Burch, a one-time colleague of Albert Bacon Fall, once made the claim that Chavez y Chavez did indeed murder the Fountains and was, in fact, murdered himself because he talked far too much about the killings and others who were involved with them.

At last count, more than twenty-five men have been identified as suspects in the murders of Albert J. and Henry Fountain. While each suspect has a host of champions, the majority of scholars today who have studied this event are convinced Gilliland, Lee, McNew, and Chavez y Chavez were all involved in the event in some way.

And what of the bodies? One of the most interesting pieces of evidence that has come forward regarding the bodies of the colonel and his son exists in a statement by Milton Ernest "Doc" Noss. Noss claimed he saw the desiccated bodies of the two individuals when he entered the famous treasure cave in Victorio Peak (see chapter 4, "The Victorio Peak Treasure Mystery"). The Noss claim, while provocative, lacks substantiation.

C. L. Sonnichsen once quoted Mrs. Bessie Voorhees, an Oro Grande, New Mexico, resident who stated that she learned "the bodies were burned in the firebox of a steam boiler." The steam boiler in question was located on Lee's ranch. Another person, unidentified, told Sonnichsen that the bodies were "buried beside a water tank and covered with concrete."

In 1900, two likely skeletons were found in a canyon in the Sacramento Mountains. While Jack Fountain, son of the colonel, held out hope that the bones would prove to be those of his father and brother, no positive identification was ever made.

In 1909, a letter mailed from Texas arrived at the Masonic Lodge in Las Cruces inquiring if there was still a reward being offered for the bodies of Albert J. and Henry Fountain. Fountain was a Mason and his lodge had offered the reward. The letter, according to Sonnichsen, was signed by a man who was once prominent in certain New Mexico affairs. When the letter writer was advised the reward was still being offered, he wrote back providing directions to the bodies he claimed were buried in a section of the Jarilla Mountains.

A search party was assembled, and Albert Fountain Jr. was invited to participate. As the party approached the region identified by the letter writer, Albert grew concerned and visibly agitated, and he broke down, stating he could not continue. He told members of the party that the discovery of the skeletons "would kill my mother." The search was called off.

In 1950, a man who claimed to be involved in the killing of the Fountains told a friend where the bodies were buried—at a high elevation in the San Andres Mountains. The site, he said, was marked by a cairn of stones. The man, whose identity was never revealed, stated that, "Upon making camp [we] drew straws to see who would murder the . . . child. One who drew the short straw quickly severed Henry's head with a knife. . . . They threw his body into a pit of alkali so that no trace would ever be found. Then, after separating, [we] agreed to rendezvous in the high San Andres where Fountain's body was buried in the most inaccessible place possible." The riders took different routes back to their homes. Periodically, the site of the grave was checked. The man who related this story said he erected the cairn of stones several years later.

In November of 1950, a search party, including three Fountain grandsons, arrived at the precise location indicated by the unidentified man. They found the cairn but no body.

Some of those who claim familiarity with this revelation and the subsequent search find reason to believe the old man may have been telling the truth. They also suggested that the stone marker might have been located a few feet from the actual burial site. In spite of their inability to find the body, and for reasons never provided, they remained convinced that Fountain's remains were buried nearby.

The case of the disappearance of Colonel Albert J. Fountain and his son Henry contains many suspects and many potential burial sites. With each passing year, more information surfaces, along with greater confusion, about motive and method. Few who have researched this event believe the case will ever be solved, but that it will go down in history as one of the West's greatest mysteries.

FOUR

✦✦✦

The Victorio Peak Treasure Mystery

In southwestern New Mexico, a rugged, weathered, rocky peak rises out of the desert floor near the center of Hembrillo Basin, a low-lying area west of the San Andres Mountains. This peak, with its origins in eons-old belowground igneous activity is somewhat remote and isolated, located at least forty miles from any significant settlement. The peak overlooks the eastern fringe of the Jornada del Muerto, a vast, waterless plain extending northward from Las Cruces for approximately one hundred miles. Bleak, steep, treeless, and forbidding, Victorio Peak is, or may have been, the location for what many consider to be the most fabulous treasure cache ever discovered in North America.

The collective mysteries relating to the origins of this treasure, how it came to be hidden inside the huge opening in the mountain, as well as its ultimate fate, have stymied researchers and historians for decades. Today, the Victorio Peak treasure continues to challenge all who attempt to study or locate it and has provided one of the most perplexing and complex mysteries ever associated with the American West.

During the sixteenth century, Spanish conquistadores and parties of prospectors and miners under the command of Francisco Vasquez de Coronado traveled, explored, and searched for precious minerals throughout much of the San Andres Mountains and the surrounding territory. Indeed, remnants of Spanish mining activity have been found in this area ever since the arrival of early white settlers. Additionally, artifacts such as pieces of armor, spurs, bridle fittings, and weapons are still occasionally discovered in the region today.

This part of New Mexico was also visited by Spanish missionaries whose intention was to establish colonies and convert the local Indians to Christianity, by force if necessary. Farming here was difficult due to

the extreme aridity, so the padres encouraged and sometimes forced
the Indians via enslavement to mine the gold and silver they found in
the nearby mountains.

During the latter part of the eighteenth century, Felipe LaRue, the
son of a wealthy French nobleman, joined a Franciscan monastery in
his native country. His reasons for doing so have long been debated,
but most agree that LaRue took the vows of poverty and chose to lead
a life of self-denial as a result of his penchant for defiance against established authority. To him, becoming a monk was a form of rebellion
against his family status and wealth.

Even as a monk, LaRue constantly challenged church authority
and often found himself in trouble with officials. As a result, LaRue's
assignments were considered less than desirable. As new missions
opened up in Spanish territories, church prelates believed it would
do the young and fiery LaRue some good to serve the faith in harsh
and primitive conditions. As a result, he was eventually assigned to a
Mexico City monastery and given menial duties in the fields.

LaRue was not in Mexico long before he returned to his old ways
and once again began challenging church policies. In response, church
officials had him whipped, confined, and sentenced to hard labor. The
more he was punished, however, the more LaRue resisted church rules
and regulations.

One day, a soldier who had been serving in New Mexico arrived at
the mission following a long journey. The soldier had fallen ill during
the last days of his travels and it fell upon Padre LaRue to nurse him
back to health. As the soldier's condition worsened, he confided in
LaRue that he had found a substantial vein of gold in the north. He
told LaRue that he planned to raise money in Mexico City to finance
a mining operation but feared he would die before he could do so.
LaRue listened carefully to the soldier's deathbed descriptions and
directions. When the soldier died, LaRue continued to think about the
possibilities of traveling to the north and finding the gold.

Following two years of continuous conflict with his superiors, LaRue
convinced a number of other monks, as well as two-dozen Indian con-
verts, to flee with him far to the north where he intended to establish
a colony and mine the gold he believed could be found. There, he
promised, the members could live and worship as they wished without
the constant strict interference of the church. Late one night LaRue
and his companions stole several mules and a quantity of supplies and
fled from the monastery. The party traveled northward toward a land

of which they had only scant knowledge. This did not deter them; all they cared about was that it exceeded the long reach of the church.

Weeks later the weary party finally reached El Paso del Norte on the Rio Grande. Here they replenished their supplies and sought information about the lands to the north before continuing. Several more days of travel brought them to Hembrillo Springs in the wide basin adjacent to the western slope of the San Andres Mountains. Here LaRue found an abundance of water and game. They were also delighted to realize the location was sufficiently isolated from main roads and, hopefully, outside intrusion.

Within hours of arriving at the basin, LaRue ordered his tired band of travelers to begin construction of a church and dwellings. As some of the men engaged in hauling stones and mixing mortar, others planted corn and beans and dug primitive aqueducts to transport the spring water to the new gardens and a hastily built cistern.

As the settlement progressed, one of LaRue's followers discovered a thick outcrop of gold in nearby Victorio Peak while hunting for game. LaRue was excited about the find and regarded it a positive sign from the heavens. With the gold, he considered, they would now be able to fashion crucifixes and chalices for use in their worship services. LaRue immediately assigned two monks to dig the gold, but as it became apparent that the ore was very rich and plentiful, two-dozen men were soon put to the task of excavating and smelting. Gold bars began to accumulate, and before long hundreds of them were stacked along the walls of the mine shaft and in a large underground chamber found inside the mountain.

Three years after LaRue fled the monastery, word of his colony and the gold mining activities somehow reached Mexico City. Intrigued by tales of the rich gold deposit, church officials sent out a force of soldiers to capture LaRue and return him to Mexico City, where he would be brought before his superiors and punished. A cadre of monks accompanied the soldiers. Their assignment was to remain at Hembrillo Basin with the Indians and oversee the ongoing mining operations and ensure that the gold ingots were shipped back to the monastery on a regular basis.

Learning of the expedition's approach, LaRue ordered the entrance to the mine closed and concealed and instructed his faithful followers to keep the location secret from the intruders.

When the contingent of soldiers and monks arrived at the settlement, LaRue was taken prisoner and interrogated about the gold.

When he refused to speak, he was stripped naked, tied to a post, and whipped until torn flesh hung from his bloody back. Despite the severe punishment, LaRue remained silent. Eventually, he lost consciousness from the brutal whippings and died the following day. Several of his companions were also tortured and killed, but none revealed the location of the rich gold mine. Finally, the discouraged soldiers chained the survivors together and began the long trek back to Mexico City, forever abandoning the little colony at Hembrillo Basin.

For almost two hundred years, Hembrillo Basin saw little human activity save for passing Indians who sometimes paused at the spring to refresh themselves and their horses. During the 1870s, Mescalero Apache chief Victorio often used the basin as a hiding place from which he would lead his warriors on raids throughout the Jornada del Muerto and the Rio Grande Valley to the west. Victorio and his band preyed on immigrants, churches, mail coaches, small settlements, and anything else that promised riches. Though the Apaches had little use for gold and currency, they had learned how desirable these things were to white men; the Indians often used gold to barter for rifles and ammunition.

Following the raids, Victorio took booty and prisoners back to Hembrillo Basin. The captives would be subjected to elaborate tortures before they were finally, and mercifully, killed. According to legend, Victorio hid the bodies of his victims, as well as items taken in robberies and raids, in the great cavern inside the peak.

On April 7, 1880, Victorio and his band, while camped at Hembrillo Springs, were attacked by a contingent of cavalry that had been tracking the Apaches for days. The Indians were successful in repelling the invaders and the nearby rocky prominence was thereafter referred to as Victorio Peak. Howard Bryan, longtime journalist for the *Albuquerque Times*, was convinced Victorio and his Apaches fought hard in order to protect the growing cache of treasure inside the mountain.

In November 1937, a group of five men and one woman, all from Hatch, New Mexico, went on a deer-hunting trip to Hembrillo Basin. While the woman remained in camp, the men decided to fan out and scout the area for signs of deer. One of the men—Milton Ernest "Doc" Noss—decided to climb Victorio Peak. From the summit he thought he would be able to obtain a good view of the surrounding plain and perhaps select a suitable location to hunt.

Noss was climbing around on the slopes of the mountain when a light rain began to fall. In search of shelter, he started making his way around some granite boulders near the top of the mountain when he spotted an overhanging rock. Believing that it would provide adequate shelter, he walked toward it. As he approached the overhang, he passed by a natural opening in the ground, a narrow fissure that appeared to extend straight down into the mountain. Ignoring the rain, Noss peered into the shaft. He discerned that, just inside the opening, the space had been widened by man; he saw chisel marks on the wall. Deeper inside, as far as the dim light penetrated, he spotted a wooden pole with notches carved into it, a kind of primitive ladder.

Later when the rain finally stopped, Noss returned to the camp and whispered his discovery to his wife. He told her that as soon as the hunting trip was over, he was going to return and investigate the opening further.

Several days later, Noss, accompanied by his wife, Ova, returned to Victorio Peak with ropes and a flashlight. Initially, Noss tried to descend the passageway using the old wooden pole ladder but found it too dangerous. With some difficulty, he lowered himself through the narrow opening using the ropes.

What Doc Noss found inside Victorio Peak that day has become one of the most controversial topics in the history of the American West. Noss's discovery has since yielded a web of intrigue, uncountable wealth, murder, theft, and a deep mystery that involved the United States Army and Air Force and some of the most prominent attorneys, military figures, and politicians in America.

According to Noss, he lowered himself some sixty feet into what he called the "shaft" where he arrived at an opening the size of a large room. On the walls of this room, he said, his flashlight revealed what he later described as "Indian drawings," painted, as well as scratched, onto the rock.

The passageway continued sloping downward at a steep angle for another 125 feet where it leveled off. After following the shaft for a short distance, Noss entered a large natural space inside the mountain, a wide, extensive rift apparently caused by a long-ago earthquake. Noss claimed the space was "big enough for a freight train" and contained several smaller rooms along one side.

Noss walked along the floor of this large chamber for several paces when suddenly the beam of his flashlight fell upon a human skeleton. Noss noted that the wrists were tied together behind the back. Before he was to leave the room, Noss would find another twenty-six skeletons, all bound and most of them secured to wooden stakes driven into the ground. Many are convinced the skeletons belonged to Victorio's victims.

In one of the smaller rooms, Noss found a Wells Fargo chest, several guns, swords, saddles, jewels, and a huge stack of leather pouches containing gold coins. Noss claimed it would take sixty mules to carry all of the pouches. In the same room he found a box of letters, the most recent ones dated 1850.

Noss filled his pockets with gold coins taken from one of the pouches, along with some of the jewelry, and returned to the large room. Against a far corner, he discovered "thousands" of bars of gold stacked like firewood. After another hour of exploration, Noss returned to the surface.

Once outside the shaft, Noss showed his wife the gold coins and jewelry and described the incredible things he had seen deep inside the mountain. When Ova asked why he didn't bring up any of the gold ingots, he explained that they each weighed over forty pounds and might prove difficult to negotiate up the narrow passageway. After a brief rest, however, he descended back into the shaft, returning an hour later with one of the gold bars.

During the next two years, Doc Noss returned to the shaft several more times and retrieved a total of eighty-eight gold ingots, each weighing between forty and eighty pounds. On several occasions he hired men to accompany him into the shaft to help remove the treasures. Benny Samaniego stated in a 1963 interview that he entered the mountain with Noss and saw "stacks of gold bars, skeletons, armor, old guns, and statues." Samaniego said all of the human remains had been tied to posts as if they had been left in the cave to die.

Another time, Noss employed a boy named Benny Sedillo. Like Samaniego, Sedillo told of seeing bars of gold in huge stacks and described how difficult it was to return to the surface carrying even the smallest of them. Sedillo also stated that Noss threatened to kill him if he ever revealed the existence of the treasure to anyone.

According to Noss, during one of his many trips into the mountain to retrieve treasure, he discovered the shriveled corpses of Colonel Albert J. Fountain and his son Henry, whose disappearance in 1896 remains one of America's greatest unsolved mysteries (see chapter 3, "The Mysterious Disappearance of Colonel Albert Jennings Fountain").

After two years of laboriously removing gold ingots, artifacts, jewels, and coins from the cave, Noss decided that his work could be made much easier if he widened the narrow opening. In 1931 he set off a charge of dynamite in the opening in an attempt to do so but succeeded in only causing a cave-in, one that completely plugged the entrance and halted any further recovery of the treasure.

Discouraged, Noss began selling some the treasure he had recovered while he considered ways of reopening the shaft. Around this time he entered into a partnership with a man named Joseph Andregg. Together, the two transported a great deal of treasure to Arizona where it was sold on the black market. The money they received, according to Noss, was to be used to finance further recovery operations.

Noss returned to Victorio Peak numerous times to try to remove the debris from the shaft, but each attempt was met with failure. He began taking his growing frustrations out on his wife and life for them became very difficult. A short time later they were divorced.

On February 15, 1946, Noss finally got around to filing a mining claim on the Victorio Peak site. After fifteen years he was still trying to find some way to break through the clogged opening. In 1949 he entered into another partnership, this time with an experienced mining engineer from Alice, Texas, named Charles Ryan. Noss showed Ryan the remaining fifty-one gold ingots in his possession, as well as several artifacts and jewels he had removed from inside the mountain. He succeeded in convincing Ryan that it would be well worth the time, effort, and expense to reopen the shaft. Noss bargained for and received a large investment of cash from Ryan.

As the two men were readying some equipment to transport to the mine, Noss discovered his ex-wife had filed a counterclaim. The matter went to court, and it was finally decided that, until the legal claimant could be determined, no one would be allowed in the area.

Noss was growing ever more frustrated with the delays and growing complications. As a result, he and Ryan argued constantly. Finally fed up with the situation, Ryan decided to withdraw from the partnership and asked Noss for the return of his investment. The request angered Noss, and he threatened Ryan. The two men exchanged blows, and during the fight Ryan pulled a gun and shot Noss in the head, killing him instantly. Ryan was charged with murder but was subsequently acquitted.

Years passed, and Ova Noss held on to her Victorio Peak claim. From time to time she would hire men to travel to the peak to try to clear some of the rubble out of the opening, but it was an expensive and difficult job and very little progress was made.

In 1955, the federal government's White Sands Missile Range extended its boundaries to include Hembrillo Basin and Victorio Peak.

When Ova Noss's employees were discovered on the range, military policemen escorted them out.

Ova Noss initiated an exchange of letters with military officials concerning her perceived right to work the claim, but they denied her access to the area for what they stated were "security reasons." Time passed, and Ova heard rumors that military personnel were attempting to gain access to the treasure chamber inside the mountain. In 1961, Ova hired four more men to travel to Hembrillo Basin to attempt to clear the shaft and try to determine the extent of military poaching on her claim.

On the afternoon of October 28, 1961, the men arrived at Victorio Peak only to discover a group of four U.S. Air Force officers and four U.S. Army enlisted men digging in the opening. The officers ordered the trespassers away, explaining they were on government property illegally.

When the men hired by Ova informed her of what they had discovered at the peak, she hired attorneys who, in turn, contacted U.S. government officials. Inquiries were made to Colonel Morton Jaffe, the judge advocate at White Sands Missile Range, but he steadfastly denied that any excavations were taking place at the site.

During the following weeks a remarkable story surfaced regarding a second entrance into the treasure room inside Victorio Peak. Three years earlier, an Air Force captain named Fiege, along with a companion, was exploring the Hembrillo Basin area when he discovered a natural opening on one side of the peak. The two men entered and followed a narrow passageway for several dozen yards. Along one wall of a portion of this access they encountered stacks of one hundred gold bars. The two men retrieved as many of the bars as they could carry.

Several years later, Fiege, accompanied by three other Air Force officers associated with White Sands Missile Range, obtained permission from the federal government to work Noss's claim. On August 5, 1961, Fiege, accompanied by the commanding officer of the range, a secret service agent, and fourteen military policemen returned to the peak, but he could not relocate the opening he found in 1959. After returning to headquarters, Fiege was given a lie detector examination that he easily passed. As a result, the U.S. Army ordered a full-scale mining operation at Victorio Peak. The subsequent activity was what the four men hired by Ova Noss stumbled onto during the visit to the basin.

Several more weeks passed, and Noss's lawyers lobbied the New Mexico state capitol in an effort to force the U.S. government to halt excavation at Victorio Peak. During the negotiations it was discovered that the acting director of the Denver mint had obtained a permit from Holloman Air Force Base Commander J. G. Schinkle that allowed him to dig for the Noss treasure. It also became clear that Judge Advocate Jaffe had been aware all along of the digging going on at the peak and purposely lied to Noss. After all of the arguments were finally heard, the Army agreed to discontinue mining operations at Victorio Peak.

In spite of the decision, the Gaddis Mining Company of Denver, Colorado, was mysteriously provided a $100,000 contract by the military to search for the Victorio Peak treasure between July 13 and September 7, 1963. As a result of around-the-clock dynamiting and bulldozing, tens of thousands of tons of rock were removed from the peak. According to the reports made available, however, no entrance was gained to the treasure room described by Doc Noss. Those who had followed the Victorio Peak controversy from the beginning were convinced that the reports were faked and that millions of dollars worth of gold and artifacts were removed from the underground chamber by military officials.

In 1972, noted attorney F. Lee Bailey was lured into the Victorio Peak case. His partners were U.S. Attorney General John Mitchell and soon-to-be Watergate figure John Ehrlichman. Bailey claimed to represent fifty clients "who knew the location of a cave with one hundred tons of gold stacked within." The clients, whose identities were kept secret, retained Bailey to find a legal way in which to remove the gold from the federal reservation. Interestingly, Ova Noss was not one of the clients.

On March 5, 1975, a federal judge ruled that the United States Army was allowed to prohibit entry into Hembrillo Basin, but that sometime in the future should try to make arrangements with the fifty claimants so they might pursue a search for the treasure.

In 1977 one such attempt was made. The army agreed to recognize six claimant groups and allowed a two-week search between missile testing operations. During the search, ground radar readings revealed the existence of a huge cavern within Victorio Peak precisely where Doc Noss said it was. The readings also revealed about four hundred feet of dirt and rock debris filling the entrance found by Noss. After two weeks, no entry was gained into the mountain, and amid numerous complaints that not enough time had been allocated for an effective search, the claimants were ordered off the range by the Army.

Not only are investigators convinced the immense treasure cache inside Victorio Peak was found and raided by military officials, they are likewise certain that the U.S. Army instigated and perpetuated a cover-up. It is also a matter of record that the Army spent hundreds of thousands of dollars conducting mining and excavation operations on and around the peak and spent a great deal of time and effort constructing roads into the area for the passage of heavy equipment. It was discovered during the 1990s that the military placed a locked steel door over the shaft discovered by Doc Noss.

It appears likely to all who have studied the pertinent facts, legend, and lore that the Padre LaRue Mine, Chief Victorio's treasure cache, and Doc Noss's discovery are all one and the same, and that they are, or were, inside Victorio Peak. There is little room for doubt that the treasure existed: several of the gold bars as well as numerous artifacts taken from the chamber have been seen, handled, and even photographed. Affidavits have been obtained from some who have seen the cache itself.

At this writing, as far as is known, there are no active mining claims on the Victorio Peak site. Roads leading to Hembrillo Basin are blocked with locked gates, and the military patrols the region on a regular basis. In recent years, private pilots conducting low-level and illegal flights over the basin have spotted military vehicles and heavy equipment on and near Victorio Peak. Direct inquiries made of military officials are ignored.

A number of historians and other interested parties are eager to attain access to the interior of Victorio Peak. The potential wealth in gold, statues, jewelry, and other artifacts that reside within does not interest them, they claim, as much as the perceived bounty of historical artifacts many believe may still be there, artifacts that could reveal much about early New Mexico history.

Today, Hembrillo Basin remains relatively quiet, save for the drone of insects and the occasional call of doves near the spring. From a distance enforced by the restrictions imposed by the United States government, many still ponder the great treasure found within the peak. Is it, or some of it, still lying in the great chamber Doc Noss stumbled into? Was some or all of it removed clandestinely by the military or members of the military without official authorization? And why won't the Army allow anyone into the area to determine what may have actually taken place?

The Victorio Peak treasure has been a mystery for at least three centuries, beginning with the activities of Padre LaRue. It continues to mystify people today.

FIVE

❖❖❖

The Lost Sublett Mine

The Victorio Peak mystery is far from being the only notable lost treasure in the American West. The West is, in fact, dotted with hundreds of lost mines and buried treasure caches. Hopeful treasure hunters continue to search for them, and a few have been found. Most, however, continue to elude seekers.

One of the most fascinating and puzzling lost treasure mysteries of the Old West is that of the so-called Lost Sublett Mine in the Guadalupe Mountains of West Texas. Often searched for, this mine reportedly once yielded great quantities of almost pure gold nuggets since the time of the early Apache Indians. When Ben Sublett found the mine in the 1880s, he extracted from it riches that exceeded the dreams of most men. That Sublett found gold is not disputed. Many had seen the ore the old man claimed was picked up from the floor of some unknown canyon. What has been, and still is, disputed is the actual location of the rich mine.

William C. (Ben) Sublett was a man almost as mysterious as his gold mine. With his death went the information pertinent to its location. Treasure hunters continue to comb the slopes and canyons of the majestic Guadalupe Mountains in hope of finding Sublett's long-lost gold.

Sublett grew up in Tennessee. He worked at a number of different jobs and distinguished himself at none. He traveled to Missouri, where he met and married Laura Louise Denny. A short time later the couple moved to Colorado, but poor luck at finding employment opportunities caused them to consider going to Texas.

By the time Sublett and his wife arrived in the West Texas town of Monahans, they were out of money and too exhausted to continue. They set up housekeeping in their wagon and a tent on the outskirts of town. Sublett worked at a variety of odd jobs while Laura took in washing.

When Sublett was not mopping out saloons or whitewashing buildings, he undertook prospecting trips to the rugged Guadalupe Mountains, located one hundred miles west of Monahans. Sublett was often warned of the hostile presence of Apache Indians in the range. Oblivious to the danger, he went anyway.

Because of his shabby dress, unshaven face, poor ways, and eccentric behavior, Sublett soon earned a reputation as being crazy. His continued ventures into the Apache-filled Guadalupes simply added to the image, and he was soon regarded as just another demented prospector. He became known throughout the area as "Old Ben."

Years passed, and Ben and Laura Sublett had three children—two girls named Ollie and Jeanne, and a boy, Rolth. As the children grew up, Old Ben and Laura were concerned that the rough-and-tumble environs of Monahans was not a proper place for them to be raised. This concern, along with the fact that Sublett had difficulty holding down a job for long, provided the impetus for the family to move to Odessa twenty-five miles to the northeast. Odessa was a growing center of ranching activity, economically viable, and provided a more suitable climate for raising children.

During the year prior to the move to Odessa, Laura began suffering from tuberculosis. Her condition grew worse with each passing week. Only six months after relocating, she died. Ollie, the oldest daughter, took over the washing business and the responsibility of raising the two younger children. As Ollie earned a rather meager living for the family, Old Ben, still unable to hold down a job for long, continued his prospecting forays into the Guadalupe Mountains. The move to Odessa did nothing to improve his reputation. With his decrepit appearance and his oft-repaired wagon pulled by two scrawny mules, he became the target of cruel jokes.

Sublett's only friend in Odessa was an elderly Apache. Like Old Ben, the Indian was constantly down on his luck and lived a hand-to-mouth existence working occasional odd jobs and taking handouts. One afternoon as the two men were whitewashing a building, the Apache told Sublett he knew the location of a rich gold placer mine in the Guadalupes. Old Ben pressed the Indian for details and was soon able to sketch a rough map of the location. With this information, Sublett's trips to the Guadalupes became more frequent, and his desire to find the gold mine grew to the point of obsession.

Sublett's extended searches caused him to further neglect his family. Eventually, several prominent townspeople encouraged authorities to place the children in the custody of others, where they could be properly cared for.

One week after efforts were begun to move the Sublett children to foster homes, Old Ben returned from the Guadalupes and changed the direction he and his family were to take for the rest of their lives. He pulled his old creaky wagon up to Odessa's Mollie William's Saloon, strode inside, and dumped a leather pouch filled with large gold nuggets onto the bar. Sublett loudly ordered drinks for everyone and announced to one and all that he had just found the richest mine in all of North America. Regarded as just another crazy prospector only one week earlier, Old Ben was now a wealthy celebrity. The following day, Sublett made arrangements for the care of his three children. He purchased new clothes for them for the first time in their young lives.

Three weeks later, Sublett returned to Guadalupes to harvest more of the gold. After a few days in the mountains, he came back with several pouches filled with nuggets. An Odessa resident described the gold as being so pure that a jeweler could hammer it out with very little effort.

Sublett continued to make frequent trips into the mountain range, always alone, always returning with pouches filled with gold. On several occasions, Odessa citizens attempted to follow him or tried to pry information about the secret location of the mine from the prospector, but Old Ben remained aloof and silent. He often reminded them that it had been only a few months earlier that they were calling him crazy.

After two years of harvesting gold nuggets from his mine, Sublett, who normally kept to himself, became acquainted with another old prospector known as Grizzly Bill. Old Ben had very few friends, and as the two men had much in common, they became close. One day Old Ben told Grizzly Bill that his secret mine contained more gold than he could ever use in a lifetime and that he wanted to share it with someone. He gave his new friend detailed directions to the mine and told him to harvest all he needed. Grizzly Bill subsequently found the mine and in a short time filled several ore sacks with the gleaming nuggets.

Grizzly Bill stopped in Pecos while returning from one of his trips to the Guadalupe Mountains, entered a popular tavern, and showed everyone his newfound wealth. He insisted on buying several rounds of drinks and initiated a celebration that lasted well into the night. At one point, Grizzly Bill, quite inebriated, was talked into a bronc-riding contest. He subsequently fell from the bucking animal and was killed instantly with a broken neck.

Sublett revealed the location of his gold mine to another friend named Mike Wilson. Old Ben showed Wilson several sacks of gold nuggets and, apparently in a generous mood, provided directions to the mine. Like Grizzly Bill, Wilson found the mine, filled his saddlebags with gold, and returned to town to celebrate. This time the celebration lasted three days, and by the time it was over Wilson discovered his gold was almost gone.

On a subsequent trip to the mine, Wilson became lost and disoriented and was unable to find it. He returned to Odessa, sought out Old Ben, and asked him for the directions once again. Sublett, incensed at Wilson's carelessness, berated him and refused to provide any information. Wilson spent the better part of the rest of his life looking for the mine he had once located. After several years of searching, he died in a small cabin in the foothills of the mountain range.

Sublett also told a man named Rufus Stewart how to find the mine. Stewart hired out on occasion as a guide for men who wanted to hunt game in the Trans-Pecos region of West Texas. One week in 1888 he was guiding several Texas and Pacific Railroad officials near the Pecos River. The hunters were after deer and pronghorn, and Stewart led them to a favorite feeding ground.

One evening after the railroad men had gone to sleep in their tents, Stewart was seated by the campfire when he heard the unmistakable jingle and creak of an old wagon approaching. Presently, the wagon pulled into the camp and the driver stepped down. Stewart recognized the newcomer as Old Ben Sublett, whom he had met several times in Odessa. Stewart had heard all of the stories about Sublett's secret mine but remained skeptical. He invited Old Ben to join him for coffee at the fire. The commotion woke the hunters, and they all came out of their tents to visit. As the night wore on, however, they returned to their bedrolls and Stewart and Sublett were alone.

Sublett told Stewart he was on his way to the mine in the Guadalupe Mountains. He confided in Stewart that this would probably be his final trip. He said he now had all the money he needed and allowed as how he was getting too old to go traipsing around in the rocky hills and canyons. Old Ben told Stewart he would take him and show him the location of the gold mine.

Stewart explained he could not leave the men he had been entrusted to guide. He also related that he was nervous about entering territory occupied by Apaches. Old Ben said the Apaches would never bother him once they saw him in his company. Though tempted by Sublett's offer, Stewart decided to remain in camp.

The following morning, Stewart fed Sublett a big breakfast and rode several miles with him toward the mountain range. Years later Stewart stated that Old Ben led him to the top of what he described as a "blue mound" west of the camp. From this mound Sublett, with the aid of a telescope, attempted to show Stewart the location of the mine in the distant mountains. After providing directions, Sublett shook hands with the guide and drove away.

Three days later, Sublett pulled into the hunters' camp on his way back to Odessa and was invited to stay for dinner. Following the meal and several rounds of drinks, the railroad men finally bedded down and Sublett and Stewart were alone once again beside the campfire.

After convincing himself that the hunters were asleep, Sublett pulled a leather pouch from the back of his wagon and poured out a quantity of gold nuggets on a small deer hide he rolled out by the fire. Stewart was stunned at the large size of the nuggets and said as much. Sublett replied that the larger ones were easier to pick up, the smaller ones were simply left on the ground. Just another rake of a hand through the gravel, said Sublett, would yield a sackful of the large nuggets.

In the morning, Sublett returned to Odessa and it was the last time Stewart ever saw him. Several weeks later Stewart, trying to remember Sublett's directions, attempted to locate the mine. Even though he made a number of trips into the range, he was never able to find the gold.

On several occasions Old Ben showed his mine to his young son, Rolth. At the time the child was unaware of its importance. Years later as a grown man, Rolth tried to relocate his father's mine, but he went to his grave without ever finding it.

Some researchers dispute the notion that Old Ben Sublett ever had a true mine in the Guadalupe Mountains. Geologists maintain that the weathered limestone that makes up most of this range is not conducive to the formation of gold ore. Gold, they state, correctly, forms when hydrothermal solutions under pressure penetrate into the rock surrounding underground pockets of molten material. No such activity has been linked specifically with the Guadalupe Mountains, but it is possible that somewhere beneath the limestone beds of what was once an extensive undersea algal reef, some evidence of volcanic activity may yet be found. This is regarded as being very likely. Within only a few miles of the Guadalupe Mountains are several other ranges that are volcanic in origin. In 1987, a geographic expedition into the Guadalupe range noted the existence of igneous intrusive rock on the southeast facing slope near where many people believe the lost Sublett mine is located.

Other investigators advance the notion that Sublett did not find a mine at all but instead stumbled onto an old Spanish gold cache left by the conquistadores who had explored this region centuries earlier. Still others believe Old Ben may have found a Mescalero Apache gold cache. Both Geronimo and Mangas Coloradas, noted Apache leaders, maintained that the Guadalupe Mountains were the source of all the gold of the Mescaleros. While the Indians had little use for such riches, they were well aware of the utility of the ore in trading for arms and ammunition.

It has also been suggested that Sublett may have participated in holdups of mail and freight wagons and that the gold was plunder from those robberies. A provocative theory, perhaps, but one that carries with it no evidence whatsoever.

Whatever the source of Sublett's gold, there is no doubt that he had access to it in great quantity. Today, well over a century later, treasure hunters come to the Guadalupe Mountains to search for Sublett's elusive gold mine. These days, much of the range lies within the boundaries of a national park and the law forbids treasure hunting. These laws, however, do not deter those who arrive with a passion for the quest, the dream, and the desire to find this lost and mysterious gold mine.

SIX

Thunderbirds

Throughout much of southeastern Utah lies an incredible array of deep, twisted canyons, mysterious caves, and amazing sandstone and limestone formations shaped by wind and water. Far from settlements and roads, many of these features are seen only by the intrepid hikers and backpackers who explore the region. Here and there among impressive geological features, the patient and enduring searcher can find hundreds of ancient petroglyphs and pictographs, many of which depict human- and animal-like forms unlike anything ever found on Earth. So fascinating and treasured are these features, both geological and anthropological, that a large percentage of this part of the state is given over to national parks, national monuments, state parks, and designated primitive areas.

In this remote and often dangerous land, the American Indian legend of the thunderbird thrives. In fact, among the hundreds of paintings on cave walls and cliff faces there can be found artistic renderings of what many consider to be the mythical and spiritual giant bird of Amerindian lore. It seems appropriate, therefore, that some of the first evidence for the actual existence of such a creature has come from that region.

This tale is composed of a number of compelling elements—buried treasure, a confrontation between a native tribe and foreign travelers, and the thunderbird. Though the historical record is scanty, the best evidence suggests that the following event took place in or around 1738. During that time, a pack train hauling hundreds of silver ingots and escorted by Spanish soldiers was traveling across a portion of southeastern Utah when it was attacked by Indians.

It is estimated thirty burros comprised the pack train, each loaded down with wealth destined for Catholic Church headquarters in

Mexico City. The precious cargo was the fruit of several Spanish-operated silver mines in Colorado and would ultimately be turned over to Church authorities, who would, in turn, place it in the Church's rapidly growing treasury. This particular pack train was only one of several that made the hazardous journey each year, hazardous because of the extreme aridity encountered, the long distances between water sources, and the presence of hostile Indians. The scattered bones of men and burros, along with the remains of packsaddles and other related gear, were sometimes encountered along the trail, reminders of the dangers of attack and thirst.

The Spanish escort, men who rode ahead, behind, and along the flanks of the pack train, kept a constant and wary eye out for Indians. Attacks were not uncommon and the loss of life was a distinct possibility.

The Spaniards were concerned that the Indians were after the silver, but that was far from the truth. The Indians cared little for this shiny metal that came from the earth, save for its occasional use as ornaments. Instead, the natives were increasingly disturbed by the continual trespass on traditional hunting grounds and holy lands by outsiders, concerns motivated by defense of territory rather than a desire for wealth.

On that particular day, as the pack train wound through narrow sinuous canyons and across open expanses of desert, it was being watched closely from hiding by a war party of Ute Indians.

The Spanish escort guided the silver-laden burros through a narrow canyon and were halfway across a broad plain when the Utes, mounted and armed, broke from hiding and launched an attack on the train. Hearing the sounds of oncoming horses and war cries from the warriors, the Spaniards looked around for shelter, a place from which they might muster a suitable defense. A jumble of weathered rocks and talus lying along the base of a nearby slope afforded only scant protection, but they rode toward it, frantically herding the heavily laden burros.

Before reaching the rocks, the party was overtaken by the Indians. A fierce and bloody, though brief, battle ensued, the result being that all but two of the Spaniards were killed. The pair of survivors somehow managed to crawl to the shelter of the rocks and had gone unnoticed by the Indians during the frenzy of battle.

As the two frightened men watched from hiding, the bodies of their companions were scalped and hacked to pieces, their dismembered parts left on the open plain. Already the corpses were attracting the attention of vultures that circled overhead in descending spirals.

According to the story related months later by the two survivors, the Indians did a strange thing. Without unpacking the silver from the burros, a contingent of warriors led the pack animals up a steep narrow path along the cliff side just behind the place where the two men were hiding. The trail led to the wide mouth of a cave into which the animals were herded. On the way to the cave, the mounted Indians and burros passed under a large painted figure on the cliff face. The image depicted in the painting was huge, and from where they lay in hiding the Spaniards could see that it was that of a large bird, its wings outstretched as if preparing to take flight.

Moments after the pack train passed through the cave opening, the two survivors heard the squeals and cries of the burros as they were being slain by the Indians. Their throats had been slashed and they were left to bleed on the dirt floor of the large chamber beyond the entrance. A short time later, the Indians rode out of the cave, down the narrow trail, and joined their fellows at the base of the cliff. After a few seconds of conversation and gesturing, the band rode away.

When they thought it was safe, the two survivors crawled from their hiding place and cautiously ascended the steep path that led to the cave. At the point where it passed under the painting of the large, fearsome bird they paused to examine it, wondering at the meaning of such a thing. Moments later, they entered the cave and found the carnage they suspected—dead burros lay randomly across the floor of the chamber, their blood already soaked into the sandy floor. The packs containing the silver ingots were still strapped to the backs of the slain animals. What was perhaps the most bizarre aspect of the scene was related to the fact that the hooves had been cut from the legs of the animals.

Months later, following a grueling journey across deserts and mountains, the two survivors finally arrived in Mexico City where they reported to their superiors and described the attack on the pack train. At first, Church authorities considered mounting an expedition to retrieve the silver from the cave, but ultimately they abandoned the scheme. According to their emissaries, the Colorado mines were nearly exhausted of silver ore and, since the Spanish were experiencing growing problems with the Indians, the Church leaders decided against sending a party of soldiers back into the area. In time, the silver mines were abandoned and the workers, soldiers, and missionaries who lived in the small communities nearby were eventually summoned back to Mexico. The testimony of the two survivors was recorded, placed in the monastery archives, and soon forgotten.

Years passed, and the story of the attack on the pack train was told and retold by many of the participating Ute warriors. Well over two-and-a-half centuries later, the account of the defense of territory against the Spanish intruders remained prominent among the Utes, a tale passed down from generation to generation via the oral tradition and linked to a number of other tribal beliefs. One of these beliefs was that if the hooves of an animal or the feet of a man were severed, the spirit was doomed to roam the earth forever and would never attain the Indian version of heaven.

The other belief was related to the large image of the bird painted on the cliff face. The bird, in a variety of forms, had appeared in Indian petroglyphs, pictographs, and carvings from coast to coast and across the North American continent. The various tribes have different names for it, but it is most commonly known as the thunderbird.

In North American Indian mythology, according to scholars, the thunderbird is regarded as a spirit, and the movement of its great wings is believed to cause thunder. During the initial phases of white settlement on the continent, the newcomers were often treated to tales about the thunderbird by the natives. The whites regarded the stories as Indian superstition and they believed such a bird could not exist. The experts said such a thing was not possible. Subsequent events at the Thunderbird Cave in southeastern Utah, however, would eventually cause the experts to shake their heads with wonder.

Hundreds of images of the thunderbird have been found throughout America since migrants from Europe arrived and undertook a gradual movement westward. Tales of the giant bird were ubiquitous. One of the first detailed descriptions of the bird came from explorer Jacques Marquette. While traveling down the Mississippi River in 1673 near the vicinity of present-day Alton, Illinois, Marquette encountered two such images on a cliff facing the river. "Their height and length inspired awe," wrote Marquette, "two painted monsters which at first made us afraid and upon which the boldest savages dare not long rest their eyes."

Marquette described the images as having horns on their heads like those of a deer, horrible red eyes, a beard like a tiger's, a face like a man's, a body covered with scales, and a long tail. And, of course, wings.

The Miami Indians, who many believed painted the figures near Alton, called this creature Piasa, which in their language means "bird that devours man." The Miami Indians, as well as other tribes, were convinced that the creature demanded sacrifices from time to time in order to keep it from preying on the community at large.

During the 1980s, a noted American treasure hunter, while conducting research in Utah, learned the story of the Ute attack on the Spanish pack train, the slaughter of the escort, and the subsequent killing of the burros in the cave. At the time, the treasure hunter believed the story was known to very few people outside the tribe, and he was convinced there was an excellent chance he might locate the cave and recover the silver ingots.

Using the vague and somewhat cryptic directions and descriptions contained in the tale, the treasure hunter spent weeks searching the vast, rugged country of southeastern Utah. And what a mysterious place he found it to be. He encountered locations with names such as Devil's Garden, Devil's Canyon, Dead Horse Point, Goblin Valley, Hoodoo Arch, The Maze, and Valley of the Gods.

After exploring hundreds of miles of the territory via vehicle, horseback, and on foot, he finally located the cave. There, on a steep cliff facing a broad desert plain was the dark opening of a cave. Making his way around and over jumbles of rock and talus at the base of the cliff, the treasure hunter encountered a steep narrow path in the rock face that led directly to the cave. After negotiating the rugged trail, one that had apparently seen little or no use during the previous two hundred years, he arrived at a point where it became somewhat level several yards from the cave opening. There, on the cliff face looming above where he stood was the painted image of the thunderbird.

The painting was that of a birdlike creature standing upright and facing the eastern side of the plain as if expecting the arrival of someone or something. Its wings were opened wide as if preparing to launch into flight. Stretching behind the figure was a long, almost reptilian tail. On the head of the thunderbird was what could be a horn, a point, or a crest. A photograph of the figure showed a winged creature that bears a remarkable resemblance to the prehistoric flying reptile that paleontologists call a pterodactyl.

But the treasure hunter was here to find treasure, not to muse about a mythical bird. After snapping several photographs of the painting, he proceeded toward the cave. Inside the large opening he found over two hundred years' accumulation of fine, loose sand that had blown in from the adjacent desert plain. The deposition of blown sand, he estimated, had raised the floor of the cave some six to eight feet above the 1738 level. He tested the floor with the tip of a shovel and was not encouraged by what he found. It was going to be difficult working in the loose, unconsolidated sand. The slightest activity stirred it, along with dust and pollen, causing it to swirl around the inside of the cave, which made breathing difficult.

A simple excavation also presented problems. Once a shovelful of sand was lifted, the fine, loose adjacent material simply slid back into the hole. In order to excavate to a depth of six to eight feet, the treasure hunter decided he would have to remove most of the sand from inside the cave, a formidable task.

The treasure hunter traveled to the nearest city where he rented a motel room and procured some supplies. Following a few days of rest and some preparation, he made the long trip back to the cave. For the next five days he labored just inside the opening, removing sand by the bucketful. Over and over he shoveled sand into two buckets, carried them to the opening, and dumped the contents down the face of the cliff.

Five days was not nearly enough time. During the course of the next three months, the treasure hunter returned to the cave several times to dig. He was beginning to believe the search for the silver was a lost cause when he made a remarkable discovery. One afternoon when he dumped a shovel full of sand into one of the buckets, the treasure hunter spotted something out of the ordinary. Reaching into the bucket, he withdrew an object, wiped the sand from it, and held it up to the light. It was the hoof from a small equine. The treasure hunter thought it might have come from a burro. Excited, he returned to his digging, and during the next two hours found several more hooves along with a number of bones. Subsequent examination determined they all belonged to burros.

An even more remarkable discovery was yet to be made. During the excavation, the treasure hunter, while anticipating encountering a great quantity of silver at any moment, barely noticed that the shovels full of sand he was digging up contained pieces of broken feathers. But these were not ordinary feathers.

At one point, exhausted and thirsty, the treasure hunter stopped to rest and noticed the shaft of a large feather sticking out of the sand near his feet. He reached down, pulled it out, and was impressed by its length and thickness. The shaft of the feather, though broken, was just over eighteen inches long and as big around as one of his fingers. The treasure hunter, an American Indian, had considerable experience with eagle and hawk feathers, but this one was several times larger than any he had ever seen before. The soft barbs that extended laterally from the shaft had, for the most part, rotted away, but enough of the structure remained such that it was unmistakably a feather from an incredibly large bird.

The feather was subsequently presented to several noted ornithologists for identification. It was determined to be a portion of a wing feather, but when later compared to one from a bald eagle, the shaft was found to be over twice as thick and would have been four times as long. What kind of bird could have yielded such a feather? Each of the experts proclaimed it came from a bird unknown to science. Further study of the feather continues.

The treasure hunter retrieved several more burro hooves and feathers, along with pieces of packsaddles, what appeared to be leather from harnesses, and a number of artifacts, but found no silver. His search for the lost silver ingots was halted when he was forced to return to his home in Georgia to oversee developments in an ongoing gold mining operation he owned there. At this writing he has not been back to the thunderbird cave.

Was the thunderbird, the so-called bird of legend, an actual creature or a mere myth? Experts tell us that much of the folklore, legend, and mythology we enjoy today have their basis in truth. Did the treasure hunter find part of the remains of an actual thunderbird? No one knows for certain. Whatever he found remains a mystery, and the feathers that came from the Utah cave continue to puzzle investigators.

SEVEN

How Did Johnny Ringo Die?

A name well known to aficionados of Western outlaw history is that of Johnny Ringo. Ringo is inextricably linked to the violent days of Tombstone, Arizona, and he and his contemporaries helped forge the enduring reputation of "the town too tough to die."

Ringo's past is shrouded in mystery, but the same can be said for many a resident of the Old West, especially those who sought to escape from troubles encountered elsewhere. Though Johnny Ringo attained a relatively high level of notoriety, his reputation as a gunman was exaggerated, and writers have suggested he may be the most overrated gunfighter of the American West. There is, in fact, no evidence that Ringo killed more than two men, although it is rumored that he killed more than a dozen Mexicans south of the border.

Not only is Ringo's past an enigma, the manner of his death—how he died and who may have killed him—remains a mystery that has troubled researchers since 1882. It remains a topic of discussion today whenever and wherever outlaw buffs gather.

Johnny Ringo showed up in Tombstone sometime during the 1870s. He claimed he came from Missouri and that he was related to the outlaw Youngers. His real name was John Ringgold and it is believed by some researchers that he came from an affluent background. Unlike other bad men of his day, Ringo had attended college, appeared to be quite literate and well read, and was known to quote poetry.

Ringo is reputed to have been involved in the famous Mason County War that took place in central Texas. From there, he wandered throughout West Texas and New Mexico for a time, occasionally winding up in jail for short periods as a result of one indiscretion or another.

Ringo was also known as a hard drinker with a short and violent temper. At six feet, three inches tall and weighing nearly two hundred pounds, he was formidable when on a drunken rampage. Once, dur-

Boothill Cemetery in Tombstone, Arizona. It was called "Boothill" because, with one or two exceptions, all buried here died of unnatural causes—with their boots on—one example of how commonplace violence was in Tombstone.
Source: Library of Congress, Prints & Photographs Division, FSA/OWI Collection, LC-DIG-fsa-8a28353

ing a drinking binge in Tombstone, Ringo overheard a man insulting a woman in the streets. Without hesitating, he allegedly walked up to the man, pistol-whipped him to the ground, and then shot him through the neck, killing him on the spot.

Ringo was a resident of Tombstone when the Earp brothers arrived and began assuming their influence over the town. Ringo never cared for the Earps, and he sided with their sworn enemies, the Clantons, the McLaurys, and Curly Bill Brocius. He especially hated Wyatt Earp's friend Doc Holliday. Ringo and Holliday confronted one another on more than one occasion, and observers predicted it was just a matter of time before the two men finally fought it out to a bloody end with their guns.

After the historic gunfight at the O.K. Corral, Ringo's hatred for the Earps intensified and he promised revenge. A number of historians have attributed the shooting of Wyatt Earp's brother Virgil to Johnny Ringo. Though he survived, Virgil Earp remained a cripple for the remainder of his life.

Several months after the shooting of Virgil Earp, Ringo, along with his friends Buckskin Frank Leslie and Billy Claibourne, went on a ten-day drinking spree. When they finally ran out of money and could no longer purchase liquor, the three men retrieved their horses and were seen riding out of Tombstone on the afternoon of July 12, 1882. Ringo was carrying a bottle as he rode, occasionally taking a sip from it. Two more bottles were packed into his saddlebags. That evening, he, Leslie, and Claibourne camped in a cedar grove a short distance outside of town.

The next morning the three men split up, with Ringo taking the road to Galeyville. A man named Billy Breakenridge said he spotted Ringo along the trail and that he was very drunk and still drinking.

Ringo's route took him by the ranch of William Sanders. Sanders waved at Ringo as he rode by and made an attempt to converse with him, but the outlaw ignored the rancher and continued riding toward Turkey Creek Canyon. About half an hour later, Sanders encountered Buckskin Frank Leslie on the trail. Leslie stopped Sanders and asked him if he had seen Ringo pass. When Sanders admitted he had, Leslie spurred his horse down the trail, seemingly intent on catching up with Ringo. About two hours after Sanders met Leslie on the trail, the wife of a rancher whose land encompassed a portion of Turkey Creek Canyon heard a gunshot.

The next day a teamster hauling a load of wood passed along the trail through Turkey Creek Canyon. Looking up from his wagon seat, he spotted a dead man seated among the limbs of a live oak tree. On investigation, he discovered the corpse was that of Johnny Ringo. The body was seated on a flat rock that had been wedged into the forks of the tree and was leaning against the trunk. Dangling from the corpse's right hand was a .45 caliber revolver, the hammer resting on an empty chamber. On the right side of Ringo's head was a bullet hole. The top of his head was blown away where the bullet had come out and pieces of brain were scattered across the tree limbs. Before the day was over, at least a dozen others would see the corpse. By that same afternoon, the sheriff of Tombstone had been informed and went to investigate.

On November 13, fourteen men who had seen Ringo's body signed a statement providing, in the estimation of the county coroner, sufficient reason to rule the cause of death as suicide. Johnny Ringo was buried a few feet from the trunk of the tree where he was found.

There are a number of mysterious elements associated with the death of Johnny Ringo.

The dead man was wearing no boots. In fact, Ringo's feet were wrapped tightly with torn pieces of his own undershirt. Since the shirt fabric was clean, Ringo apparently did not walk anywhere after the strips of cloth were attached to his feet.

Ringo's horse was missing. The mount was eventually found a few days later six miles away in Sulphur Springs Valley. One of the outlaw's boots was found on the ground nearby. The other boot was never located.

Yet another strange discovery was the fact that Ringo's cartridge belt was fastened around his waist upside down. Had he, or someone else, taken it off and reattached it in a hurry?

If Ringo had shot himself in the head at such close range, powder burns would have been evident. None of the fourteen witnesses or the coroner mentioned the existence of powder burns. In fact, a few observers commented on the absence of same.

Some have speculated that the bullet that killed Ringo came from the empty chamber found in his revolver. The truth is, many a Western gunman, for reasons of safety, commonly left the hammer resting on an empty chamber. Though Ringo's gun was found thus, there was no evidence that a shot had been recently fired from it.

Perhaps the most bizarre observation of all was the fact that, after Ringo was dead, someone had attempted to scalp him.

Breakenridge went on record as supporting the suicide theory. In his opinion, a very drunk Johnny Ringo had dismounted in the shade of the tree, removed his boots, tied them to the saddle, and lay down to sleep off his hangover. The horse, suggests Breakenridge, wandered away, and Ringo awakened to find himself with no horse, no boots, and no water. Breakenridge hypothesized that Ringo tore his undershirt up, wrapped his feet, and set out in search of water. Despondent, and crazed from thirst, continued Breakenridge, Ringo climbed into the tree and shot himself. Breakenridge also stated that Ringo's revolver had dropped from his hand and had gotten caught on his watch chain.

Breakenridge's observations have been deservedly criticized. Indeed, his entire credibility as it relates to Ringo's death has been maligned. For one thing, Ringo could not have been crazed by thirst since a clear running stream was located only a few feet from the tree in which he was found. Writer Jack Burrows noted that Ringo could have dived into the stream from the point where he was found. Burrows further states that if Ringo "possessed the capacity to draw his pistol and shoot himself, he also possessed the capacity to fall forward into the stream." In fact, there was evidence that Ringo had to cross the stream to get to the tree.

Regarding Breakenridge's comment about the gun being caught on the watch chain, the statement filed by the coroner reads that the gun was "grasped in the right hand."

During several periods of despondency that Ringo was known to suffer, he was heard to threaten suicide. Few people who knew him, however, believed he was capable of the act. His closest friends maintained that he never would have attempted such a thing.

Growing numbers of researchers don't believe Ringo committed suicide. One theory that has gained considerable support over the years advances the notion that the outlaw was killed by Buckskin Frank Leslie. Leslie has been placed in the area at the time by rancher William Sanders and was apparently in pursuit of Ringo. It was discovered several years later that Leslie had been paid by the Wells Fargo Company, who reputedly suspected Ringo of robbing them and wanted him dead. Furthermore, while serving time in prison several years later, Leslie admitted to a jailer that he killed Ringo.

Other researchers insist that Johnny O'Rourke should be considered a suspect in the killing of Ringo. O'Rourke was a two-bit gambler described as an "insignificant runt" and nicknamed "Johnny-Behind-the-Deuce." Importantly, O'Rourke had a motive for killing Ringo. After being arrested for killing a man in Charleston, Arizona, O'Rourke was nearly lynched by a mob led by Ringo. The gambler swore revenge. Eventually, O'Rourke was transferred to the jail at Tucson. Shortly thereafter, however, he escaped and was never seen again.

It has been written by Earp biographer Stuart Lake that Wells Fargo agent Fred Dodge employed the escapee O'Rourke as an undercover informer. According to Lake, Dodge, a trusted agent, claimed O'Rourke told him he encountered Ringo by chance in Turkey Creek Canyon. While the outlaw was sleeping off a drunk in the shade of an oak tree, O'Rourke crept up, shot him through the head, and placed his body in the tree. The statement by Dodge, by all accounts an honorable man, has authority and a ring of logic.

Some believe Wyatt Earp killed Ringo. It is well known that the two men hated one another, and either would likely have taken advantage of any opportunity to kill the other.

One such opportunity presented itself to Earp. Acting on a lead, Earp allegedly tracked Ringo after the outlaw rode out of Tombstone with Leslie and Claibourne. It is believed by some that as Earp was tracking Ringo down the Galeyville Road, the latter was setting up camp in Turkey Creek Canyon. After building a fire, it has been hypothesized that Ringo pulled off his boots and tied them to his saddle. In his later years, Earp reportedly stated that when Ringo spotted him, the outlaw grabbed his pistol and ran up the canyon barefooted. Suffering from the rocks and thorns, he pulled off his undershirt, tore it into strips, and tied them to his feet. Earp followed Ringo up the canyon, killed him, dragged the body back down to the camp, and placed it in the tree where it was found the following day.

This version of Ringo's death is unlikely for several reasons. The principal source of this tale comes from a writer named Frank Lockwood, who claimed to have interviewed Wyatt Earp about the incident. Lockwood, however, is regarded as one who often exaggerated events and is generally not provided much credibility by serious researchers.

On the other hand, another researcher/writer named John D. Gilchriese has brought to light a hand-drawn map sketched from memory by Wyatt Earp. The map, according to Gilchriese, precisely locates the spot where Earp claimed to have shot Ringo and where he placed his body in the tree.

Earp's presumed role in the death of Ringo is fraught with problems. One is related to logistics. Earp had been living in Colorado, where he was just prior to Ringo's death and immediately afterward. For Earp to travel from Colorado to Turkey Creek Canyon and back, in addition to finding the time to track Ringo down, suggests an unlikely journey of approximately six days.

The final word on Earp's involvement in Ringo's death, according to some, may have come from Josephine Earp, who related her husband's role in Ringo's death in the book *I Married Wyatt Earp*, edited by Glen Boyer. A rather skeptical writer named Burrows accuses Mrs. Earp of having literary ambitions and that her account is more one of fiction than fact. In recent years, author/editor Boyer has come under severe criticism from respected researchers for making up all or portions of the Josephine Earp manuscript.

The Earp account is difficult to take seriously for two other reasons. For one thing, if it were true that Ringo had tied pieces of undershirt to his feet and ran up the canyon, the fabric would have been soiled. It was not. According to witnesses, the cloth was clean. For another, the pieces of Ringo's brain that were splattered onto the same tree trunk prove that he was shot at that location and not somewhere up the canyon.

There is yet another theory regarding the death of Johnny Ringo, and that is that it came at the hands of Doc Holliday. On January 17, 1882, both Ringo and Holliday were arrested and fined thirty dollars each for bitterly quarreling on the streets of Tombstone. After Ringo's body was found, a rumor circulated around Tombstone that Holliday was the killer. The rumor has refused to die.

Johnny Ringo was thirty-two years old when he met his end. The mysteries surrounding the circumstances of his death have intrigued researchers for well over a century. It is unlikely that the truth will ever be known.

EIGHT

The Multiple Mystery
of Warren Earp's Death

On the evening of July 6, 1900, Warren Earp and Johnny Boyett engaged in a heated argument in the Headquarters Saloon, Willcox, Arizona. Before the evening was over, Earp, unarmed, was dead from a gunshot wound to the heart. Boyett was never charged with the killing.

In spite of the testimony of several witnesses who allegedly observed the shooting, it remains unclear to this day how Warren Earp met his death. Furthermore, something that has never been explained is the reason for the haste involved in disposing of Earp's body. Additionally, many still wonder if Warren Earp's death was a revenge killing for an event that occurred almost twenty years earlier, something that he, in truth, had no part in.

Warren Earp's death would be of no interest to anyone were it not for the fact that he was related to Wyatt Earp and the rest of the notorious Earp brothers. Warren was the youngest of the brood. He was also the least active of them, having missed the violence and bloodshed in the Tombstone of the 1870s and the so-called gunfight at the O.K. Corral. Unlike his brothers, Warren, as far as anyone knows, never shot anyone.

Warren was born in Pella, Iowa, on March 9, 1855. When he was twenty-two years old, Warren accompanied his parents on a move to San Bernardino, California, where he worked for several years as a clerk in his father's grocery store. In 1882, Warren traveled to Tombstone and for the next ten years accompanied his older brother Wyatt on his travels throughout the West.

In 1891, Warren returned to Arizona and took a job as a stagecoach driver on the Willcox-Fort Grant run. Two years later he went to work for the Cattlemen's Association as a range detective. Eventually, he settled into a job as a bartender in a Willcox saloon.

On July 4, 1900, Willcox was bustling with activity, as cowhands from surrounding ranches arrived in town for a holiday celebration. One of the cowboys was Johnny "Shorty" Boyett, foreman of the nearby Sierra Bonita Ranch. Years earlier, Boyett and Earp had both been on the payroll at another ranch—Boyett as a cowhand and Earp as an undercover inspector. It has been said that Earp sometimes bullied the smaller Boyett and that the two fought with each other on several occasions.

On the evening of Friday, July 6, Earp and Boyett both entered the Headquarters Saloon at the same time. The two jostled one another in the doorway and began arguing. Earp, pointing a finger at Boyett, loudly accused him of being paid a bounty to kill him. Boyett reportedly held out his hands in a peaceful gesture and told Earp he didn't want any trouble.

Angry, Earp commanded Boyett to go get a gun. Boyett told Earp he was not afraid of him, turned on his heel, and walked across the street to the Willcox House hotel. Boyett entered the hotel, went behind the registration desk, and retrieved two pistols. When hotel owner W. R. McComb asked Boyett why he was taking the guns, the foreman said he might need them before the night was over.

Boyett returned to the Headquarters Saloon and stalked through the front door carrying a pistol in each hand. According to witnesses, Boyett called out for Earp, calling him a son of a bitch. Boyett then spotted Warren Earp in the doorway that connected the saloon with the adjacent restaurant. Boyett immediately fired two shots but missed Earp by a wide margin. Earp ran to a side door and exited into the street.

Upset at missing his target, Boyett then fired two shots through the saloon floor. Seconds later, Earp reentered the saloon from the same door through which he had just left. Eyewitnesses claimed Earp held his coat open to show he was unarmed and then started walking toward Boyett. Twice Boyett called out for Earp to stop, but he kept advancing. When Earp was within a few feet of Boyett, the cowhand fired, apparently sending a bullet through the heart of Warren Earp. He was dead before he hit the floor.

A sheriff's deputy arrived moments later and inspected the body. He found no weapon save for a half-opened penknife. Boyett was placed under arrest, and Earp's body was carried to the office of M. J. Nicholson, the town physician. Following a hasty examination, the body was buried in the town's cemetery within only three hours of the shooting. Nicholson later testified before the coroner that the bullet entered Earp on the left side and ranged downward.

Following a short hearing, Boyett was released from custody on the afternoon of the next day. Judge W. F. Nichols determined there was no cause to indict Boyett for a crime, and if there were, no jury in the land would convict him.

For those who have studied the killing of Warren Earp, there remain a number of puzzling aspects to the case. First, it was never explained how Boyett, a relatively short man at only five-feet-six-inches tall, could have shot downward into Earp, who was at least six inches taller. Some who have examined the specifics of the event suggest that the trajectory of the bullet through the body implies Earp may have actually been seated when shot. Witnesses to the incident, however, maintained that Earp was standing in front of the killer. Nevertheless, the path of the bullet, as described by the physician who examined the body, suggests that the witnesses were mistaken.

Second, a few have speculated that Earp may have been shot, not by Boyett, but by someone who was standing on the second floor landing and shooting downward at the target. The angle of the path of the bullet through the body offers some support for this contention.

Third, it is also perplexing why Earp, who was unarmed, continued to approach Boyett after being warned and after clearly seeing that his adversary was pointing two pistols at him.

Fourth, and perhaps most troubling of all, is the fact that Earp's body was disposed of so quickly. Not only was the corpse buried in haste, but no marker was placed on the grave.

There also exists some disagreement over the reasons for the killing of Warren Earp. Some have dismissed it merely as the result of an ongoing grudge between him and Boyett, but others are not so certain.

Some researchers have suggested that Earp's death was the culmination of a two-decade-old plot for revenge, a plot that involved a number of people including some Willcox residents. It is suspected that Boyett may have been paid to kill Warren Earp by men who suffered at the hands of the Earp brothers in Tombstone during the 1870s, men with a grudge who wanted revenge no matter how long it took to achieve it.

The judge who released Boyett, it has been suggested, was likely involved. Otherwise, there was no reason to release the prisoner with the assumption of what a jury would decide. The hurried burial, as well as neglecting to place a marker on the grave, provides fuel for the conspiracy theory.

Though Warren Earp at the time amounted to no more than what one writer refers to as "a two-bit badman," it is possible that he may have been killed for no other reason than that he was related to Wyatt, Virgil, and Morgan Earp.

Advancing some support for this theory, an Arizona newspaper article that appeared on July 11, five days after the shooting, stated that Warren Earp's killing was the result of a feud that had "existed between Boyett and Warren Earp," and had its origins in the bloody warfare between the Earp brothers and the cattle rustlers in south-eastern Arizona during the 1870s. Another article appeared in a San Bernardino, California, newspaper that stated Warren Earp was a victim of a feud that had its origins twenty years earlier.

If it is true that Warren Earp died as a result of a feud between the brothers and others, then it was a feud he had no part in, for he didn't arrive in Arizona until long after the troubles were over. On the other hand, it has long been believed that some men were simply committed to wiping out the entire Earp clan.

Warren's brother Wyatt stated that it was a clear case of murder. Wyatt was convinced that a number of people were involved and believed it was related to revenge. Wyatt, along with brother Virgil, eventually traveled to Willcox to investigate the killing.

Some researchers believe that Wyatt and Virgil caught up with Boyett and murdered him, but substantive evidence is lacking. What is known, however, is that Boyett was never seen again.

Was the killing of Warren Earp part of a plot? Were the Willcox judge and other citizens involved in it? The details of Warren Earp's death will likely never be known, nor is there any way to identify all of the people involved. Too much time has passed since the act, witnesses are long dead, and records are hard to come by.

Mystery and controversy have surrounded the Earps since their time in Tombstone and have followed them throughout their lives. Despite the years that have passed since they died and were buried, the mystery and controversy will not go away.

NINE

The Disappearance
of Buckskin Frank Leslie

Buckskin Frank Leslie was glamorized by writer Walter Noble Burns as a notorious gunman and credited with killing fourteen men. The truth is, Leslie was known to have killed only three people—two men and one woman. Somehow Leslie earned an exaggerated reputation as a shootist, and he was, in fact, feared by most men who came in contact with him. Very little is known about Leslie. Several attempts have been made to fill in the gaps in his enigmatic life over the years but documented research is sparse.

Even more mysterious is the fate of Frank Leslie. When he was released from prison in 1896 he simply vanished. For the next sixty years, however, reports surfaced that he had been spotted in California, China, and Alaska. One report had him living in Kentucky. In the end, no one really knows.

Buckskin Frank Leslie first came to public notice shortly after he arrived in Tombstone, Arizona, in 1880. He claimed he was a former scout with the U.S. Army, a claim that has never been proven. Leslie, whose real name was Nashville Frank Leslie, dressed himself in fringed buckskins in the manner of George Armstrong Custer. In spite of what he described as an illustrious career that yielded fame and fortune, he took a job as a bartender in Tombstone's Cosmopolitan Hotel.

Two weeks after arriving in the desert mining town, Leslie killed a man. Leslie was courting the estranged wife of fellow Cosmopolitan Hotel bartender Michael Killeen. During a break, Leslie and May Killeen were visiting quietly at a table in a dark corner of the bar when Mr. Killeen approached them. On two previous occasions, Killeen had warned both his wife and Leslie to stop seeing one another. This time there was no warning; Killeen attacked Leslie, knocking him to the ground. During the subsequent exchange of blows, Killeen pulled a pistol and fired at Leslie, striking him twice in the head but inflicting only superficial wounds. When a friend of Leslie's tried to break up the fight, Killeen began beating on him. Patrons began herding the three men outside the bar and into the hotel lobby where the fighting resumed.

Two more shots were fired, this time by Leslie. One hit Killeen in the left cheek, the other in the abdomen. After a night of terrible suffering, Killeen died the following day. Two weeks later, Killeen's widow and Leslie were married.

Leslie's violent and volcanic temper, more than his prowess with a gun, earned him a reputation as a tough and remorseless killer. In addition to his willingness to shoot at the slightest provocation, references attest to his incredible accuracy. One account stated that Leslie could hit a fly on the wall at twenty paces. Another story is told that noted gunman Doc Holliday, on being confronted by Leslie, backed down and walked away. When he was drunk, which was almost all of the time, Leslie would make his new wife stand against a wall while he fired his revolvers at her, outlining her body with bullet holes.

In November 1880 Leslie quit his job at the Cosmopolitan and went to work as a bartender at the Oriental Saloon that was, at the time, co-owned by Wyatt Earp. During his employment at the Oriental, Leslie was deputized by the Tombstone City Council and given authority to make arrests on the premises.

Though Leslie worked for Earp, he also courted favors with Earp's enemies—the Clantons, the McLaurys, Curly Bill Brocius, and Johnny Ringo. Some researchers claim Leslie may have had a role in goading the separate factions into violence, and might have been responsible for the famous gunfight at the O.K. Corral.

Leslie spent a great deal of time hanging around with Ringo and Brocius. At the same time, yet unknown to everyone, Leslie was being paid as a Wells Fargo informant. Years later, Fred Dodge, a Wells Fargo agent, stated that the company actually offered Leslie a handsome sum of money to kill Ringo. Johnny Ringo was reported to have robbed Wells Fargo shipments on more than one occasion.

Though controversial, a handful of researchers maintain that the mysterious death of Johnny Ringo can be attributed to Buckskin Frank Leslie.

During the second week of July 1882, Ringo, outlaw Billy Claibourne, and Leslie spent most of their time drinking at a number of Tombstone establishments. On the afternoon of July 12, Ringo climbed on to his horse and rode out of Tombstone toward Galeyville, another mining town located several miles away. Ringo took the Barefoot Trail that wound past the ranch of William Sanders before turning into Turkey Creek Canyon. Sanders waved at the outlaw as he rode by and even tried to engage him in conversation, but Ringo was too drunk.

Several minutes later Sanders watched Buckskin Frank Leslie come down the same trail as though he was following Ringo. Later that same afternoon, a resident of Turkey Creek Canyon heard a gunshot. Around evening of the same day, Leslie was seen riding his road-weary horse into Tombstone.

At the time, several Tombstone residents, as well as some subsequent researchers, believed Frank Leslie murdered Johnny Ringo. A coroner eventually ruled the death a suicide, a judgment supported by a statement signed by fourteen of Tombstone's leading citizens.

Among those who were convinced Ringo was killed by Leslie was Ringo's friend Billy Claibourne. Claibourne entered the Oriental Saloon while Leslie was tending bar and, cursing and threatening loudly, challenged him to a fight. Hotel employees quickly hustled the young outlaw out of the bar and into the street. Standing outside the bar, Claibourne shouted at Leslie that he intended to get even. With the threat, he turned and walked away.

Several minutes later a citizen informed Leslie that Claibourne was returning and this time he was carrying a rifle. Leslie reached under the bar and retrieved a Colt .44 revolver with a twelve-inch barrel, stepped out a side door, and crept toward the front corner of the saloon.

As Claibourne approached the front door to the bar, Leslie stepped out into the street and ordered the young outlaw not to shoot his weapon. As several witnesses looked on, Claibourne wheeled around at the sound of Leslie's voice, raised the rifle, and fired. The shot missed Leslie by a wide margin, and the former scout calmly pointed the revolver and shot Claibourne in the chest.

Just before he died that afternoon, Billy Claibourne stated to the doctor attending his wound that Buckskin Frank Leslie had admitted to him that he killed Johnny Ringo.

For reasons never understood, Leslie quit his job as bartender in the
Oriental Saloon after killing Claibourne. Following this, he spent most
of his time drinking and philandering.

With the passage of several months, Wyatt Earp, along with his
surviving brothers, left Tombstone. Many of the major and minor
participants in the town's violent heyday also departed. Eventually
the mines closed down, the miners left, and several businesses that
depended on the miners went broke.

Of all the participants in Tombstone's violent days, only Buckskin
Frank Leslie remained. At various times he worked as an army scout,
a customs inspector, and a ranch foreman. In 1887, May Killeen
divorced Leslie, and a short time later he took up with a saloon girl
named Mollie Williams.

Williams was, among other things, a dancer at Tombstone's Birdcage
Theater. She was tall, blonde, leggy, and very good-looking. When
Leslie met Williams she was living with the theater's owner, E. L.
Bradshaw. In fact, Mollie Williams sometimes used the owner's last
name as her own. After observing Leslie's apparent interest in Mollie,
Bradshaw warned him to stay away from the Birdcage. Two weeks
later, Bradshaw's body was found on a nearby creek bank. He had
been murdered "by assailant or assailants unknown."

The Birdcage Theater.
Source: Library of Congress, Prints & Photographs Division, Historic American
Buildings Survey/Historic American Engineering Record/Historic American
Landscapes Survey Collection, HABS ARIZ,2-TOMB,18-1.

A few days later, Williams moved in with Leslie. On the few occasions they were seen in public during the next two years, they were either drunk or fighting.

On July 4, 1889, Leslie commenced a week of drinking in Tombstone's various saloons. At first Mollie joined him, but after becoming frightened at his tendency to pull out his revolver and shoot at anything, she decided to return to their cabin.

After Mollie left, Leslie tried unsuccessfully to pick fights with several different Tombstone citizens. Finally he retrieved his horse from the livery, mounted up, and rode out of town, firing his pistol along the way.

What happened when Leslie arrived at his cabin has long been debated. Some claim that when he walked in the door, Mollie confronted him with a loaded pistol. Others maintain Leslie caught her in the arms of a ranch hand named Johnny Neil.

On entering the house, Leslie shot Mollie in the chest, killing her instantly. Turning toward Neil, he shot twice, striking the young man in one arm and in the stomach. Moments later, Leslie passed out drunk.

Though badly wounded and in great pain Neil crawled more than a mile to a neighboring ranch and reported what had occurred at Leslie's cabin. The rancher sent one of his hands into Tombstone to fetch the sheriff and a doctor.

By sunrise the sheriff, accompanied by three deputies and the doctor, were riding out to Leslie's cabin. To their surprise, they met Leslie riding toward them. Leslie told the sheriff that Neil had killed Mollie, and in self-defense he was forced to shoot Neil. The sheriff did not believe Leslie's story and placed him under arrest.

At his trial, Buckskin Frank Leslie pled guilty to the murder of Mollie Williams. On January 10, 1890, he was shipped to the Yuma Territorial Prison to begin a seven-year sentence.

Two months after being admitted to the prison, Leslie attempted an escape but was quickly apprehended and placed in solitary confinement. Apparently learning his lesson, he subsequently became a model prisoner, worked in the prison pharmacy, and aided the prison physician in caring for the sick. Leslie got along well with the prison guards, and one, Frank King, became a close friend.

During his time in prison, Leslie lobbied for clemency and somehow convinced a number of prominent Arizona citizens to write letters to the governor on his behalf. On November 17, 1896, Leslie was granted a full pardon. Two weeks later, he married a wealthy divorced socialite named Belle Stowell.

Following the wedding, Leslie agreed to an interview with a reporter from a local newspaper. During the interview he stated that he and Belle planned to travel to China for their honeymoon. The following day, Frank and Belle Leslie checked out of their hotel, boarded a westbound coach, and were last seen riding across the Colorado River bridge into California. Nothing was ever heard of Buckskin Frank Leslie again, at least nothing that was ever substantiated.

Two years after Buckskin Frank Leslie was released from the Yuma Territorial Prison, former guard Frank King stated that during his incarceration, Leslie had confided in him that he killed Johnny Ringo.

City records for San Francisco, California, for the years 1904 and 1905 show that a man named Frank Leslie was employed as the manager of a grocery store. It was never verified if it was the outlaw.

In 1920, a California newspaper ran an interview with an elderly man who claimed he was the famous Buckskin Frank Leslie. During the interview, the old man admitted that he had killed Johnny Ringo.

In 1922, another California newspaper reported that documents found on the body of a man who committed suicide in the hills to the east of San Francisco belonged to the outlaw Buckskin Frank Leslie. The documents have never been authenticated.

During the late 1920s, reports came from the Sierra Madres of Mexico that Buckskin Frank Leslie was living there and working as a ranch foreman. In 1933, Leslie was reported seen in Alaska where he was supposedly operating several successful mining claims.

In 1948, an old man lay dying in a San Diego hospital. He was known to friends and acquaintances as Barney McCoy. Visitors came and went, many of them bringing cards and flowers to the elderly fellow. Just before he died, Barney McCoy pulled his attending physician close to him and whispered that McCoy was not his real name. He told the doctor that he was known as Buckskin Frank Leslie, had lived for many years in Tombstone, Arizona, and had killed several men. Following the old man's death, no attempts were made to verify his claim, and today his records cannot be found. It was estimated that in 1948, Leslie, if alive, would have been around ninety years old.

Sometime during the late 1950s, a strange letter was received by an unidentified man. The three-page letter was postmarked Russellville, Kentucky, and detailed many of the events that took place in Tombstone during the 1880s. The writer of the letter had intimate knowledge of people, places, and events, knowledge that could only have been gained as a result of having been there at the time.

The letter writer claimed to be 106 years old. The letter was signed—Buckskin Frank Leslie.

TEN

❖❖❖

How Did the Catalina Kid Die?

Ferdinand Walters led an active outlaw life for several years in Alaska before arriving in the southeastern Arizona border town of Nogales. Tiring of a somewhat less-than-successful career of banditry and constant pursuit and harassment by law enforcement authorities above the Arctic Circle, Walters, who assumed the nickname "the Catalina Kid," became a full-time gambler.

Following a confrontation one evening in Nogales's Palace Saloon where Walters shot and killed three people, he walked out into the street. A moment later the Catalina Kid was dead, and to this day controversy swirls around what actually happened. Some writers contend Walters committed suicide, but others maintain he was shot and killed by someone else.

Ferdinand Walters regularly occupied a table at the Nogales Palace Saloon, where he conducted card games. The life of a gambler, he was often heard stating, was a significant improvement over his previous career as an outlaw. Years earlier in Alaska, Walters had been a member of the notorious Soapy Smith Gang that terrorized Skagway and the surrounding area. The gang robbed, extorted, and sometimes killed the unfortunate victims. While Walters made a few headlines in Alaska, he was considered only a small-time and somewhat insignificant outlaw in Arizona. Walters often gambled for twenty-four hours straight without stopping. His manner of dress was curious for the southwest—he was seldom seen when he wasn't wearing a black suit and black vest and sporting a long black cape that flowed behind him when he walked. His black hair and drooping black moustache added to his dark and mysterious manner. It was well known that Walters regularly smoked opium and was sometimes known to interrupt card games so he could retire to a nearby opium den for an hour or two.

Walters was allowed to conduct games by Palace Saloon owner
M. M. Conn. Conn was an astute businessman, generally well known
and well respected by Nogales citizens, was known as a fair and honest
man, and was polite and courteous to all who entered his establishment.

Conn kept a wary eye on Walters. He often heard whispers that
the Catalina Kid was running a crooked card game and this deeply
concerned the honest Conn. Conn, however, had no proof at the time
that the gambler was cheating. When Conn informed Walters of the
rumors, the gambler became angry and demanded to know the source
of the accusations, but the owner refused to tell him.

Walters, who was normally high-strung and sensitive, grew irritated
and suspicious of everyone who played cards with him. One evening
Conn finally determined that Walters was indeed cheating. Specifically, after watching the gambler for several hours, he determined that
the Catalina Kid was using a marked deck. Conn confronted Walters
with his suspicions and fired him on the spot. Incensed and insulted,
Walters complained loudly to any and all who would listen to him, but
it did no good. In spite of his termination by Conn, however, Walters
continued to come into the Palace Saloon during the evenings to drink.

One night while visiting the Palace, Walters was stunned to discover
that Conn had replaced him with J. J. Johnson, a Nogales gambler
known as "Cowboy." Walters had long detested Johnson. Before the
evening was over, Walters learned that Johnson had been the one to
inform Conn about the marked cards.

During the time the Catalina Kid was running the table at the Palace
Saloon, Johnson was one of the few gamblers who experienced any
success playing cards with him. During the games, Johnson kept up
an aggravating chatter, constantly needling Walters and driving him
to distraction.

After discovering that Johnson was now conducting the card games,
Walters came to the Palace every night thereafter. He drank heavily,
downing one whiskey after another, and constantly glared at the poker
table where Johnson played cards. Walters grew increasingly irritated
and, from his barstool, occasionally hurled insults at Johnson and
Conn. One evening, Walters had to be forcibly removed because of
this threatening manner.

A few nights later while playing cards down the street at the nearby
Monte Carlo Saloon, Walters stated to the other three gamblers that
he was going to produce a few dead men before the sun rose on the

morrow. Walters had been drinking a lot, and his fellow gamblers attributed the threatening boast to too much liquor.

As the game wore on Walters lost heavily, and with each turn of the cards became more and more agitated. Around 3:00 AM, Walters threw down his cards and excused himself from the table. Walking out into the street, he headed to the nearest opium den where he spent forty-five minutes smoking.

After leaving the opium parlor, Walters returned to the Monte Carlo Saloon and stood and glared at the card players for several minutes. Presently, he wrapped his cape tightly around his torso, turned, and strode out of the saloon.

A few minutes later, Walters stomped into the Palace, glared at Johnson and Conn, and ordered a ham sandwich. On receiving the sandwich, he placed it in his coat pocket. Turning toward the card table, he stared for another minute at Johnson who was smiling as he raked in a large pot. Sliding off the barstool Walters, visibly drunk, half-walked and half-staggered the few paces to Johnson's table and stopped directly in front of the gambler. Pulling a .45 caliber Colt from a holster under his coat, the Catalina Kid raised the weapon, pointed it at Johnson's head, and pulled the trigger. The bullet made a hole between the gambler's eyes and he died immediately.

Walters wheeled around and frantically scanned the saloon as if looking for someone or something. Eventually, his eyes came to rest on owner Conn who was seated at a table in the far corner. Realizing Walters meant to kill him, Conn bolted from his chair and ran toward the front door. Walters fired again, the bullet passing through Conn's head just behind his right ear and shattering the glass door beyond.

Turning again, Walters pointed his revolver at the closest target. This time it was another gambler named George Spindle. Just as Walters jerked the trigger, Spindle slapped his gun hand, knocking the weapon aside and avoiding certain death. The bullet pierced Spindle's hat and powder burns seared his face. Fearing Walters would shoot again, Spindle dropped to the floor and feigned death.

Looking around, Walters pointed the weapon at another gambler named Modesto Olivas. Frightened, Olivas dropped his cards and started to rise from the chair. Before he reached his full height Walters fired, sending a bullet through Olivas's forehead and killing him instantly.

Calmly, with his weapon dangling loosely from his hand, Walters turned and walked out the front door of the saloon. Once he reached the middle of Morley Street, according to one newspaper account the following day, the Catalina Kid raised the revolver to his head and blew his brains out.

A rival newspaper quoted Dave Black, a regular Palace Saloon patron, as stating that as he ran through the front door in pursuit of Walters, he saw the Kid raise the gun to his head and fire.

In spite of the two eyewitness accounts, however, the death of the Catalina Kid manifested a number of curious elements. Jess Marleau, a Nogales businessman, heard the shooting and ran toward the Palace Saloon. Because it was dark, he did not see the body of Walters in the street; he walked by it and passed through the barroom door. Inside, Marleau saw the dead Conn lying on the floor at his feet and the frightened Spindle fleeing out a side door. Blood was puddling under Cowboy Johnson's head where he lay next to the card table.

A moment later the sheriff arrived. While he examined the bodies in the saloon, he asked Marleau to go outside and ascertain whether Walters was dead or alive. As Marleau approached the figure lying in the middle of the road, he could hear Walters coughing out his final breaths. Blood gushed from his mouth and his eyes bulged from his head. A moment later he was dead. Marleau searched the body and the street for several feet around the corpse but could not find the Kid's revolver.

One-half hour later, Walters's weapon was found by a passerby. It was lying next to the wood-planked sidewalk in front of the saloon and several yards from the body. During the subsequent confusion of the investigation, however, the gun mysteriously disappeared. Before it did, it was whispered around the Palace Saloon that only four cartridges were missing from the weapon. Three of the bullets were responsible for the deaths of Johnson, Conn, and Olivas, and the fourth nearly killed Spindle. If Walters had committed suicide, a fifth bullet should have been missing. While Walters's weapon may have only been fired four times, all of the witnesses testified to hearing a total of five shots.

The Catalina Kid died and was buried in 1905. His death, however, remained shrouded in mystery until 1956. In that year, a researcher who was examining a collection of journals, diaries, and papers at the Arizona Historical Society encountered a reference to the Nogales killings that shed considerable light on the matter.

Found among the historically significant documents was a statement by a man named Billy Bowers, who was quoted as saying that the Catalina Kid had been killed by Dave Black. Black, it will be remembered, was the so-called witness who was primarily responsible for the notion that Walters committed suicide. Bowers related that, immediately after the shooting, he watched Black remove a gun from a drawer behind the bar, run outside, and shoot Walters in the head. In addition to himself, Bowers claimed that several other witnesses saw Black kill Walters, but no one ever said anything because they did not want to get their friend in trouble. Researchers have suggested that the Kid's revolver may have been misplaced on purpose in order to protect Black.

Dave Black himself also provides a bit of mystery. Three years following the shooting he went mad and was committed to the Arizona Territorial Insane Asylum. Some writers claim Black died inside the asylum a few years later. Others insist he escaped and fled to California. The truth may never be known.

ELEVEN

Whatever Happened
to the Outlaw Bill Smith?

Like many other killers and bandits of the day, outlaw Bill Smith never received the notoriety and headlines as did more famous Western bad men such as Billy the Kid, Jesse James, and Butch Cassidy. Smith, though well known throughout much of Arizona and New Mexico, simply never attracted the attention of the journalists and dime novelists, those scribes who related semi-authentic but mostly made-up fables of life and outlawry in America's Wild West.

In spite of the fact that Smith was comparatively unknown as far as outlaws go, he was no less deadly and dangerous than his counterparts. After several years of stealing livestock, killing men, and traveling down an outlaw trail that would no doubt have placed him in the annals of famous outlaws, Bill Smith vanished without a trace, and researchers continue to wonder at his fate.

Outlaw Bill Smith was described by Arizona newspapermen as "handsome." He stood over six feet tall in his boots, was muscular with strong features, and possessed black, piercing eyes that could "cut straight thorough to your soul," stated one writer. The only flaw in his appearance, according to descriptions, was a noticeable gap between his front teeth.

Bill Smith turned to outlawry at a relatively late age. He worked most of his life as a cowpuncher on Arizona and New Mexico ranches and was thirty-five years of age when he decided making money would be much easier on the other side of the law. He assembled a gang consisting of several men who shared his philosophies, including his three brothers—Al, Floyd, and George.

Cattle rustling was the specialty of the Bill Smith gang, but the outlaws also found profit in stealing horses and robbing travelers. As they carried out their activities they were responsible for the killings of several men, including at least one Arizona ranger.

In 1898 Bill Smith was arrested for cattle rustling and placed in the St. Johns, Arizona, jail to await trial. Brother Al, pretending to be an attorney, smuggled a gun into Smith's cell and the next day the outlaw broke free. For the next three years neither cow nor horse nor traveler was safe in eastern Arizona and western New Mexico as the Bill Smith gang ranged far and wide.

One day in March 1900, St. Johns sheriff Ed Beeler received word that a group of men were spotted butchering a steer not far from town alongside the road to Springerville. Suspecting it might be the Bill Smith Gang, Beeler quickly organized a posse and hurried out to the site.

About three miles southwest of town, the posse rode up on the five men who immediately stopped their butchering and opened fire on the lawmen. After several minutes of exchanging shots, with not a single person struck, the outlaws mounted up and rode away, leaving the partially butchered beef behind. The posse set out in pursuit.

Learning of the shootout and the possibility that the Bill Smith gang was in the area, nearby rancher Dick Gibbons assembled several of his cowhands and joined Beeler the following morning to assist in the chase. Gibbons selected four of his men—Antonio Armijo, Frank Leseuer, Francisco Ruiz, and his nephew Gus Gibbons—to ride ahead of the main posse, ferret out the outlaws, and drive them back toward the sheriff and his men. By midmorning, there was no sign of either the outlaws or the cowhands, so rancher Gibbons and the rest of his followers headed down the trail in the direction taken by the rustlers the previous day.

After riding about a mile, rancher Gibbons spotted Armijo and Ruiz approaching on horseback. The two men told Gibbons that while they stopped to rest their horses at one point along the trail the previous night, Gus Gibbons and Frank Leseuer continued to ride ahead. That, according to Armijo, was the last time they had seen the two men.

Knowing that his nephew and Leseuer were significantly outnumbered by the outlaws and concerned they may have been the victims of an ambush, the anxious Gibbons spurred his mount forward, his men following close behind.

One hour later, Gibbons arrived at the edge of a shallow canyon and scanned the narrow valley below. Within seconds, the rancher spotted a dead man lying on the hillside near the wash. A short distance away was another body. After several more minutes, Gibbons finally located a winding trail that led to the bottom of the canyon. He approached the first body and saw it was that of his nephew. The young man had been shot three times in the head and most of his face was blown away. The other body, as Gibbons suspected, was that of Leseuer.

After examining the signs, Gibbons concluded the two ranch hands had been ambushed as they followed the outlaws, shot from only thirty feet away. They were robbed of their wallets, guns, and hats.

Later that evening, the Bill Smith Gang struck again. After riding hard to Reserve, New Mexico, sixty miles to the southeast, the outlaws stole a number of fresh horses and continued to flee toward the Chiricahua Mountains. By now, several posses had been mobilized and an extensive manhunt was on.

One such posse was led by U.S. Marshal George Scarborough, at the time best known for his capture of the outlaw Pearl Hart. On the afternoon of April 3, 1900, Scarborough was convinced he was following the trail of the Bill Smith Gang. For reasons never explained, Scarborough selected only Deputy Walter Birchfield to accompany him and ordered the remaining posse members to conduct a search in another direction several miles away. Scarborough and Birchfield continued following the suspicious tracks that led directly to Triangle Springs, an isolated location in the Chiricahua Mountains. Having learned nothing from the killings of Gus Gibbons and Frank Leseuer, the two lawmen rode straight into an ambush.

Approaching the springs, Scarborough and Birchfield were suddenly surprised by a dense volley of gunfire coming from nearby rocks and trees. Scarborough was struck in the leg during the first few seconds of the fight, the bullet shattering a bone and knocking him from his horse. Deputy Birchfield was hit in the arm but rode directly over to where the marshal lay on the ground. Dismounting, Birchfield stacked up rocks around Scarborough to form a low wall of protection. Behind the rocks, the two men continued to exchange shots with the outlaws.

When darkness descended on the canyon Birchfield, though in great pain, slipped away from the protection of the wall and crawled through brush and rock until he located his horse. After mounting up, he rode off in search of the rest of the posse. By the time he found them several miles away, a snowstorm had struck the region. In the ensuing hard-driving snowfall, the tired lawmen hurried back to Triangle Springs. By the time they arrived, however, the outlaws had fled. The posse found Scarborough still hiding behind the rocks, suffering mightily from his wound. With all haste, the marshal was transported to Deming, where his leg was amputated. He died a short time later.

Before the week was over, a reward of $2,000 was offered for the capture of the outlaw Bill Smith. Months passed, but no sign or word of Smith and his companions appeared.

Rancher Dick Gibbons remained troubled by the killing of his nephew, but he was also bothered by the growing rampant lawlessness permeating Arizona. Citing the need for more and better law enforcement, Gibbons ran for the Territorial Legislature, won handily, and set about establishing the Arizona Rangers. The Rangers were formally organized in March 1901, and one of their first assignments was to bring in Bill Smith.

On October 3, 1901, the Bill Smith Gang struck again. After stealing a large herd of horses they fled into the hills south of Springerville. Carlos Tafoya was the Arizona ranger stationed in the area, an assignment that carried the priority of keeping an eye out for the Smith Gang. In a very short time, Tafoya assembled a posse and went in search of the outlaws.

After following the gang and the stolen herd south of Fort Apache to the Black River in Arizona's Graham County, Tafoya finally spotted their camp late one afternoon. It was located in the bottom of a wide, shallow wash. The ranger moved the posse some distance back up the trail so they wouldn't be seen or heard. During the remaining two hours of daylight, Tafoya formulated a plan to capture the outlaws.

Just before sundown, the lawmen set out on foot and quietly made their way to the western rim of the wash. Tafoya decided on this strategy so that, once the shooting started the outlaws would be looking into the intense glare of the setting sun. The decision, while sound in theory, proved to be a foolish one for Tafoya and his men.

At the appropriate time Tafoya and one of the posse members, Bill Maxwell, rose up. Maxwell, who had once been a friend of Bill Smith, called to the camp below and ordered the outlaws to surrender. Smith and his gang responded by grabbing their rifles and opening fire at the silhouettes of the lawmen starkly highlighted on the ridge. Maxwell was struck in the head by a bullet and died instantly. Tafoya was stuck twice in the midsection and placed out of action. Leaderless, the rest of the posse scattered for cover as Tafoya cried out for help.

During the shooting, the outlaws' horses spooked and fled down the wash, leaving the rustlers afoot. With no gunfire coming from the frightened posse, the outlaws fled up the wash on foot toward the nearby mountains.

The following day another posse was formed, this time a large one. It was led by a tough ranger named Mossman. They soon found and followed the tracks of the Bill Smith Gang into the high mountains but eventually lost them in the fresh fallen snow. They searched the area for the next two days but found no signs of the outlaws.

As the years passed, rumors circulated throughout Arizona and New Mexico that outlaw Bill Smith and his brothers had been spotted in Mexico. According to a former Arizona ranger, Bill Smith's mother told him that soon after the gunfight with Tafoya's posse, her sons fled to Galveston, Texas, where they boarded a ship to Argentina. Some Smith researchers accept the mother's story as true, but others are convinced she made up the tale to deliberately mislead the lawmen.

Though Bill Smith was never seen again following the shootout in Graham County, he was heard from. Several months following his escape, Smith apparently learned that one of the lawmen killed during the fight was his old friend Bill Maxwell. A short time later, Smith sent word to Maxwell's mother stating that he was unaware Bill was a member of the posse. He explained that the death was an accident and offered his apologies.

Smith also wrote a long letter to Arizona Ranger Mossman, explaining in great detail the events of the shootout in the wash. The letter contained no return address or readable postmark.

While some remain convinced that Smith fled to Argentina with his brothers, others claim to have evidence that, years later, Smith returned to the Springerville area and, using a different name, eventually became a respected citizen.

The truth? No one knows for certain. Maybe no one ever will.

TWELVE

◆◆◆

Pearl Hart, Female Outlaw

Compared to males, the ranks of famous female outlaws in America's Old West are rather thin with only a few notable women listed. Life was difficult for the average woman who lived in the sparsely settled West; the work was arduous and endless, the dangers plentiful, and neighbors were few and far between. Daily toil and hardship caused women to age quickly. Childbirth and disease took a heavy toll. And it has been written that loneliness probably killed many more.

A few of these early Western women sought escape from the dawn-to-dusk drudgery of trying to maintain a household. A large percentage of them simply returned to their previous homes in the east. Some became prostitutes. And a few became outlaws.

Belle Starr is regarded by many researchers as the most famous of the Old West female outlaws. Starr, by all accounts, was a successful horse thief and, according to her biographers, a stagecoach robber. It has been said, though never proven, that she robbed trains.

Two other outlaw women rode with the famous Doolin Gang—Jennie Stephens and Annie McDolet, better known as Little Britches and Cattle Annie. Along with the Doolins, these two bold women rustled cattle.

Less is known of Pearl Hart, a colorful, diminutive stagecoach robber turned activist and actress. Her outlaw adventures were relatively short-lived, but they served to catapult her to a significant level of notoriety and fame. Then she dropped out of sight. Mysteriously, she reappeared twenty years later, but like smoke in the wind she vanished once again from public view, this time forever. What eventually became of Pearl Hart has never been learned.

It is believed that Pearl Hart was born Pearl Taylor around 1877 in Ontario, Canada. Life for Pearl began in a family so poor that her widowed mother was unable to provide adequately for her children. Pearl and her siblings were sent to live with relatives and friends. After being passed around to various aunts and uncles for several years, Pearl finally ended up in a boarding school. The young girl despised the institution and the strict, vindictive matrons who ran it. At the first opportunity, she ran away.

The chance to leave the boarding school was provided by a man named Hart, a young gambler who lost at cards as often as he won. Hart has been described as rail-thin with a sallow complexion. In the style of gamblers of the day, he sported a pencil-thin moustache, a black frock coat and vest, and a black, straight-brim hat.

Hart proposed marriage to the sixteen-year-old Pearl, and, after eloping, the two traveled throughout parts of Canada and the United States living in cheap hotels and camping in a ragged tent along the road. To earn a living for himself and his bride, Hart gambled when he had the opportunity, but he was seldom successful. His gambling was compulsive and he lacked the skill to win consistently. In addition to cards, Hart bet on the horses as well as other sporting events, but winning regularly at these pursuits also eluded him. Eventually, Hart began drinking heavily, staying drunk for several days at a time. Pearl, tiring of Hart's drinking and inability to earn a living, left him.

After several weeks of tracking her, Hart located Pearl and asked her to go to Chicago with him to make a new start. The young woman, now pregnant, agreed to the proposition and in 1893 the two checked into a seedy hotel not far from the fairgrounds where the World's Columbian Exposition was taking place.

While attending the Exposition, Pearl became fascinated with the displays and oratory relating to life and times in the American West. There, she believed, lay her destiny, and she began imagining what it would be like to live there. Utterly charmed, she returned to the hotel, gathered up her few belongings, and fled to Colorado, abandoning Hart in Chicago.

Arriving in the bustling mining town of Trinidad, Pearl initially found work as a boardinghouse cook and later as a maid. A few months after arriving, Pearl gave birth to a son. With the youngster in tow, she moved south and west to Arizona where she settled in Phoenix and held down jobs as a cook, waitress, housekeeper, and barmaid.

Two years after leaving Chicago, Pearl was quite surprised when husband Hart showed up one day. The gambler was repentant, promised to change his ways, and asked Pearl to take him back. At first she resisted but finally relented, and the two lived together for another three years. Life, however, was not smooth for them. Income was irregular and sparse, and another child, a girl, was born. Despite Pearl's pleadings, Hart continued losing money at the gaming tables and horse races. Seized with the frustration of his considerably less than successful occupation, Hart sought relief once again in drink. During his drunken stupors, which came more often than ever, he turned mean and sometimes beat Pearl and the children.

Pearl was disappointed in Hart's behavior. She grew fearful he would hurt the children so she sent them to live with her mother in Canada. Shortly thereafter, tired of the abuse and poverty, she decided to leave Hart once again. This time, Pearl fled to New York.

The tenacious Hart followed her. After another two years of alternately fighting and living together, the two eventually returned as a married couple to Arizona, this time settling in Tucson.

Once back in Arizona, however, Hart reverted to his old ways: gambling, losing, and drinking. One evening after suffering a severe beating at the hands of Hart, Pearl decided she had had enough and was determined to leave him once and for all. When she went to retrieve her savings, she discovered her husband had stolen them. In the dark of night and taking with her only the clothes she wore, Pearl Hart ran from their home and hitched a ride to Phoenix where she moved in with a former employer.

Within a few weeks of Pearl's departure, Hart joined Teddy Roosevelt's Rough Riders and left for training somewhere in the east. The year was 1898.

In Phoenix, Pearl reflected on her miserable life and regarded herself as a complete failure. She attempted suicide several times and even failed at that.

While working as a cook in Mammoth, Arizona, Pearl met and became friends with a man named Joe Boot. Boot eventually secured a better job for her as a maid at a boardinghouse in the mining town of Globe, about eighty miles east of Phoenix. Consistent with Pearl's bad luck, the mines closed down a short time later and she found herself out of work.

While trying to decide what to do with the rest of her life, Pearl was surprised once again by the sudden appearance of Hart, who had been given an early discharge from the army. This time she sent him away, but not before giving him all of her money.

Financially destitute, as well as physically and emotionally drained, Pearl Hart roamed the streets of Globe searching for work and contemplating suicide once again. When she was convinced that her luck could get no worse, she received a letter from a family member telling her that her mother was dying. With no money, Pearl was unable to travel to her childhood home to be with her mother during her last days. Brokenhearted and with little hope of surviving, she decided to borrow a gun and shoot herself in the head.

Before Pearl found the opportunity to kill herself, Joe Boot invited her to accompany him to his mining claim. She agreed to go and as a result became excited about the opportunity to become involved digging ore from the rock with him. Together the two worked long hours each day for nearly two months. At the end of that time, however, they had not retrieved enough ore to pay their bills.

During this time, a few researchers hypothesize Pearl and Boot became romantically involved. Some claim they already were. Still others maintain Boot simply assumed the role of a fatherly protector. It is unlikely the truth of the relationship between the two of them during this time will ever be known.

Though never proven, it has been maintained by some that Pearl and Boot entered into a scheme to rob and kill innocent men. Posing as a prostitute, Pearl allegedly invited men to her quarters where Boot, hiding in a closet, would sneak up on an unwary customer and bludgeon him with a mallet. After relieving the victim of cash and valuables, they disposed of the bodies in a nearby stream. Since most of her victims were presumed to be miners and thus without much money, the two eventually abandoned this scheme in favor of another.

Pondering their future while dining on the last of their provisions one afternoon under a shade tree, Boot suggested to Pearl that they rob a stagecoach. Initially Pearl was appalled at the idea, but in desperation agreed if Boot would promise not to hurt anyone.

On the afternoon of May 30, 1899, Pearl Hart and Joe Boot waited behind some trees and rocks in Cane Springs Canyon outside of Globe. Just as the coach came into view around a nearby bend, the two, riding horses and wearing masks, moved out into the road and raised their pistols, pointing them at the driver. Pearl was wearing male clothing and had her hair cut short.

The driver reined his team to a halt and, without having to be told, raised his hands above his head. Three passengers were ordered out of the coach and told to do likewise. Pearl dismounted and took possession of the weapons carried by the passengers. This done, she told them to place their money and valuables on the ground at their feet. As they did so, Pearl took the driver's handgun and placed it in her belt. As Boot stood guard, she scooped up a total of $431 and stuffed it, along with watches and rings, into her pockets. After a moment, she returned a dollar to each of the victims and ordered them back into the coach. Pointing his gun at the driver, Boot told him to continue on down the road and not look back. Pearl Hart and Joe Boot had just pulled the last recorded stagecoach robbery in the United States.

Knowing that the driver would report the robbery at the next stop, Pearl and Boot decided to ride into the nearby mountains in an attempt to elude the posse that was certain to trail them. All night long they traveled and became lost several times. So disoriented were they that when morning arrived, they rode out of the hills only to find themselves directly across from the place where they had robbed the stagecoach the previous afternoon.

By now a posse had picked up their trail and was only a few miles behind the inexperienced and inept robbers and was closing. As they fled, Pearl and Joe encountered a number of setbacks that cost them valuable time. One night when they crawled into a cave to get some sleep they were chased out by a wild boar. During most of their flight, unusually heavy rains fell and made travel difficult and uncomfortable.

On one occasion when the two robbers were fording a rain-swollen stream Boot, growing weary, fell from his horse and nearly drowned. Finally, after three days of little or no food or rest, the two stopped in a grove of oak trees, turned their horses loose to graze, and fell asleep. Just before sunrise, their pursuers found them, crept up to the sleeping pair, and awakened them at gunpoint.

Until then the lawmen believed they were tracking two men and were startled to discover one of their quarry was a woman. After having their hands tied behind them, Pearl and Joe were helped into their saddles and, accompanied by the posse, led to Benson, Arizona, one hundred miles to the south.

During the ride, Pearl related the details of the robbery and flight. Her story captivated the lawmen who listened in quiet, rapt attention throughout much of the trip. From Benson, Pearl and Joe were placed on a train and transported to the jail at Florence. Though Boot remained quiet about the stagecoach robbery, the small woman, surprised and flattered by the attention she was receiving, continued to relate an account of her adventure. In time she became a celebrity in Florence. As one writer dramatically phrased it, she was "a symbol of contemporary western womanhood, driven to desperation by love and a dying mother."

Pearl grew emboldened. At the trial she told the prosecutor she preferred not to be tried under laws that members of her sex had no voice in making. Her boldness inspired other women, and her story was told in newspapers throughout the country. The growing suffragette movement regarded her as a heroine, and her name and deeds were told and retold by thousands.

The continuing and growing attention Pearl Hart was receiving at the Florence jail became so troublesome that the sheriff finally had her sent to Tucson where she was incarcerated in the Pima County courthouse.

Adding to her now heady and growing reputation Pearl, along with a fellow inmate, escaped from the courthouse and fled to New Mexico. Once there, she began assembling a gang of outlaws and made plans to rob trains, banks, and stagecoaches. Around this time she posed for a photograph. The image portrays the tiny Pearl wearing a man's clothes and standing with her left foot propped up by an overturned bucket, a Winchester across one knee, and a revolver in her belt. Just as Pearl was about to launch her career as the bandit queen of the Southwest she was recaptured and returned to Tucson.

A few weeks later Pearl was shipped back to Florence where she awaited trial. She was incarcerated in a jail cell next to Joe Boot. During the time they spent there, it was reported the two fell deeply in love.

Boot was tried, found guilty of robbery, and sentenced to thirty years in prison. After he was sent away, Pearl never saw him again. Pearl fared better at her trial. Although she was positively identified as one of the robbers by the driver and passengers and, though she never denied her participation in the holdup, Pearl was acquitted after the jury deliberated only ten minutes.

Shocked and dissatisfied with the verdict, the judge ordered the government prosecutor to charge Pearl for stealing the stagecoach driver's pistol. Intimidated, the jury subsequently found her guilty of the charge and the judge sentenced her to five years at the Yuma Territorial Prison.

The sentence turned out to present more problems for the state of Arizona than anyone could have anticipated. For one thing, Pearl was the only female prisoner in the institution and special arrangements were necessary for her care.

For another, Pearl began conducting religious services and speaking out on the evils of crime. In the process, she converted several of her fellow inmates to Christianity. Her speeches incited not only the other prisoners, but the citizenry of Arizona and much of the rest of the country as well.

Yet another problem surfaced during Pearl's incarceration—she became pregnant. The only men known to have visited her were a locally prominent minister and the governor of Arizona. As a result of this embarrassing predicament, Pearl Hart was quietly pardoned by the governor in 1902 after serving only one-and-one-half years of her sentence. She emerged from prison a national celebrity once again. Only days after she was released, Pearl Hart traveled to Kansas City to live with her sister. Before Pearl arrived, her sister made arrangements for a stage production of Pearl's life, with Pearl herself in the leading role. A few months later the play opened to large crowds, but after only a few days, poor attendance caused it to close down.

One of many posters for the circus-like Buffalo Bill's Wild West shows— one of many places Hart was rumored to have fled.
Source: Library of Congress, Prints & Photographs Division, Courier Litho Co., LC-USZC4-2350

Disappointed at the lack of success and growing weary of the attention, Pearl Hart grew reclusive, seldom speaking to anyone and rarely venturing out of her Kansas City home. Some claimed she left Kansas City and never told anyone where she was going.

Nothing has ever officially been heard from or about Pearl Hart again. Rumors circulated that she worked as a prostitute in Kansas City, Denver, and Trinidad. Some researchers maintain she rode with the Buffalo Bill Wild West Show, but no records could be found to substantiate this claim.

In 1904, a woman named Pearl Hart was arrested in Kansas City for a minor offense, but no details were made available and no one knows for certain if it was the same woman. A year or two later, a poem relating Pearl's outlaw adventures was sent to a Kansas City newspaper. The poem allegedly bore her signature and it was printed, but it failed to arouse any interest in the now largely forgotten would-be bandit queen of the Southwest.

After the poem appeared in the newspaper, nothing more was heard from Pearl. Neither relatives nor friends knew where she might have gone or what became of her.

In 1924, a gray-haired woman, estimated to be in her late forties and walking with slightly hunched shoulders and a pronounced limp, entered the Pima County Courthouse in Tucson. She asked the receptionist on duty if she could be allowed to walk around and look over the premises. When the receptionist asked her why, the woman told her that she once lived in the building many years ago.

The stranger and the receptionist toured the courthouse together and conversed for a while. The stranger told the young woman that it looked very much like it had in 1900. Before the woman left, the receptionist asked her name.

"Pearl Hart," said the stranger, who then turned and walked out of the building. She was never seen again.

Over the years other rumors surfaced. One had Pearl married to a rancher in Globe and living a relatively happy life and finally passing away in her nineties during the 1960s. Though several researchers attempted to determine the truth of this rumor, nothing was ever verified.

Whatever happened to Pearl Hart remains an unsolved mystery, one that historians and researchers still try to unravel.

THIRTEEN

❖ ❖ ❖

Who Killed Belle Starr?

Myra Maybelle Shirley was born on February 5, 1848, near Carthage, Missouri. During the forty-one years of her life, she became heavily involved in horse stealing and a number of other illegal activities. She was married four times, each time to an outlaw. Starr eventually acquired the sobriquet "Bandit Queen of the Wild West."

Belle's father was John Shirley, a Virginian by birth who moved to southwest Missouri shortly after marrying. He became a well-known and well-respected horse breeder, miner, and trader, as well as a tavern owner and noted Confederate sympathizer. John Shirley made certain his daughter Belle was properly educated and sent her to the Carthage Female Academy. Despite her subsequent penchant for stealing horses, Belle was well read and an accomplished piano player.

Belle's youth was marked by a number of influences that undoubtedly shaped her future as an outlaw. Her father's passion for and support of the Confederacy led to a number of clandestine meetings with Rebel fighters and spies at his Missouri tavern. During such gatherings, Belle overheard numerous firsthand accounts of Yankee atrocities. Belle's brother was killed during the War Between the States, an event from which some researchers claim she never recovered. At an early age, Belle became well acquainted with noted outlaws. Frequent visitors to her home were Frank and Jesse James and the Younger brothers. With her growing hatred for the Union, it is believed by some that Belle delivered information about federal troop movements in Missouri to the Confederates.

A short time following the killing of her younger brother, Belle's family moved to Texas, settling not far from Dallas. In 1866, Belle married James C. Reed, a noted outlaw of the day. Some historians claim she married Reed because he killed the man who shot her brother. No evidence in support of this contention, however, has ever

A scene titled "Jesse James' Reception," no doubt depicting the James-Younger Gang. Jesse and Belle shared a common hatred for the Union and tendencies for lawlessness.
Source: Library of Congress, Prints & Photographs Division, LC-USZ62-2174

been found. Most believe Belle was merely impressed by Reed's bravado and relished the opportunity to be free from parental restraints. From this union, Belle gave birth to a daughter, Rose Lee Reed, who was called "Pearl," and a son, Edwin. Some writers have claimed Pearl was fathered by the outlaw, Cole Younger, a frequent visitor to the Reed household. Younger denied it.

While it has never been verified, some believe that Belle often rode with her outlaw husband Reed and occasionally helped him rustle horses and rob trains.

Following the killing of two men, Reed was forced to flee from Texas. He traveled to California, and Belle, along with the two children, joined him several weeks later. After living for a brief time in the Golden State, outlaw Reed moved his family back to Texas.

During the time she was previously living in Texas, Belle began taking on the persona with which she was identified throughout most of the rest of her life. She often wore a Stetson hat with a long ostrich plume extending rearward. A fringed buckskin jacket was worn over velvet dresses and a brace of revolvers was usually strapped to her hips. Belle was known to be bad-tempered, loved to drink and gamble, and could out-curse any muleskinner in the region. While there is no evidence that Belle ever committed murder, she was not afraid to fire her revolver at anyone who angered her. She apparently feared nothing and no one and never backed down.

When Jim Reed was killed near Paris, Texas, in 1874, Belle took the children and moved to Rich Hill, Missouri, and lived there for a short time with her late husband's mother.

In 1880 Belle apparently forced Bruce Younger to marry her. According to most references, Bruce was a cousin to Cole Younger and lived with Belle following the death of Reed. Once formalized, the union lasted only a few hours before Younger fled, never to be seen alive again. Several years later, it was reported, his mummified body was discovered in a cave in New Mexico.

Three weeks after Younger left, Belle married Sam Starr, a Cherokee Indian and a notorious horse thief and whiskey peddler. Starr was a feared outlaw who had also killed many men. He wore the dried earlobes of his victims strung onto a leather cord that dangled from his neck.

Belle and Sam, along with Belle's children, moved into Starr's cabin at Younger's Bend on the Canadian River in Oklahoma. Younger's Bend was visited often by the James Gang, the Daltons, the Youngers, and other outlaws, all of whom found hospitality and refuge with Belle. It is believed that Belle became heavily involved in horse stealing during this time. In 1883, Belle and Sam Starr were each sentenced to one year in prison by Judge Isaac C. Parker. Belle was released after six months.

In 1886, Sam Starr was killed by lawman Frank West, who also died in the shooting. With Sam dead, Belle's claim to the Indian lands on which she lived was in jeopardy. After contesting the issue for several years, she simply decided to marry another Indian and eventually wed Jim July, a Creek.

By now Belle was growing famous as a result of fictional and exaggerated treatments of her outlaw ways. Relishing the notoriety, she made July, who was fifteen years younger than Belle, change his last name to Starr. According to neighbors, Belle often treated July as if he were little more than a hired hand.

As an outlaw, Belle was overrated, and her fame, or infamy, came about mostly as a result of adventure-filled dime novels that contained little truth but that sold widely throughout much of the American East. Outside of a handful of outlaws, Belle had very few friends but a lot of enemies. As a result of making a number of threats, she was roundly despised by many residents in the Younger's Bend area.

The greatest mystery with regard to Belle Starr's life is her death. For several days prior to her killing she confided in neighbors that she was having premonitions about her death and feared that some of her enemies were about to catch up with her.

Belle Starr met her fate on February 3, 1889, along a stretch of dirt road that wound alongside a field belonging to a neighbor named Edgar Watson. She was returning to her cabin after a visit to a friend when a shotgun blast exploded from behind a corner fence post about twenty feet away. Belle was struck in the back and neck with a load of buckshot that knocked her from her saddle. As she tried to rise from the road, muddied from recent rains, her assailant climbed over the fence, approached the prone woman, fired another round of buckshot into her shoulder and face, and then fled.

One of the first to reach the mortally wounded Belle Starr was her daughter, Pearl. As Pearl leaned close to her mother, Belle whispered something just before dying. Pearl never revealed what Belle said. To this day, no one is certain who killed Belle Starr, and at least seven individuals have been identified as suspects.

One suspect was the younger brother of her former husband, Jim Reed. Many believed the brother was convinced that Belle had been responsible for providing information to lawmen that eventually resulted in the killing of Reed. Some claim the brother quietly moved into the Younger's Bend area, lived under an assumed name, and awaited the opportunity to slay Belle. No concrete evidence, however, was ever forthcoming to support this contention.

Another suspect was Tom Starr, the father of Belle's third husband, Sam. Tom Starr was convinced Belle had been responsible for Sam's death. Shortly before Belle was gunned down, Tom Starr was heard to state that "Belle would never cause another killing." Despite the implied threat, Tom Starr was never given serious consideration by law enforcement authorities as a possible assailant.

One of the posse men who tracked and captured horse thief Jim July was certain Belle's widower was also her murderer. Bob Hutchins, one of the deputies who investigated the death of Belle Starr, came away convinced that Jim July was the murderer.

A local farmer, Milo Hoyt, told Hutchins that July approached him and made him an offer of two hundred dollars to kill Belle. Hoyt refused and July, growing angry, rode away saying, "Hell, I'll kill her myself and spend the two hundred on whiskey." Hoyt believed July wanted Belle dead because she found out about his dallying with another woman in a nearby community. Others have claimed July wanted Belle dead because he was convinced she was having affairs with several men.

Farmer Edgar Watson told Deputy Hutchins that it was his shotgun that was used in the murder, but that Jim July pulled the trigger. Watson claimed July came to his house to borrow his shotgun to shoot a wolf that was killing some chickens. July returned the shotgun later that evening, said Watson. Both barrels had been fired.

July was never charged with the killing, and he continued on his lawless ways. While being arrested several months later, July was wounded by the same deputy, Hutchins, and died three days later.

Belle's neighbor Hy Early may have had reason to murder the Bandit Queen of the Wild West. During the fall of 1888, Early complained often and bitterly to neighbors that Belle had stolen some of his horses and cattle. Belle learned about Early's accusations and one day several weeks later when she met him on the road, fired her rifle at him, narrowly missing his head. Belle told him if he made any more foolish statements she would kill him.

Within hours after the incident, it became common knowledge in the area that Early had offered seventy-five dollars to anyone who would kill Belle Starr. One day following her death, Early and Pony Starr, one of his cowhands, were riding toward Starville when a man named Bertholf rode up to them. Addressing Early, he told him he had come for his money. Early reached into his saddlebags and counted out seventy-five dollars in gold.

A growing number of writers and historians believe Belle Starr's killer was Jim Middleton. For his entire life, Middleton was convinced Belle Starr and Jim July killed his brother, John. Shortly after robbing the Creek Nation of $16,000, John Middleton rode with Belle and July on a trip to Dardanelle, Arkansas. Fearful that they might encounter lawmen on the trail, John, according to Belle, left them near the Poteau River, stating that he was going to take a back route around Fort Smith. Several months later, John Middleton's remains washed up on the riverbank, and Jim was certain that Belle killed him for the money. According to an old friend and Younger's Bend landowner Claude Hamilton, Jim Middleton summoned him to his bedside as he was dying in 1938 and confessed he shot Belle to avenge his brother's death.

The aforementioned Edgar Watson was the first and only person arrested for the killing of Belle Starr. Watson was a ruggedly good-looking man with red hair and a beard, stood six feet tall, and was a relative newcomer to the Younger's Bend area. Belle and Mrs. Watson became friends, and the latter confided in Belle that her husband came to the region after fleeing Florida where he had been charged with murder.

Belle and Watson eventually had a falling out. Ill feeling prevailed, and Belle threatened to tell authorities about some of Watson's illegal activities. Investigators stated that the tracks around Belle's body matched Watson's footprints. The prints were followed onto Watson's property and detectives lost them about one hundred yards from Watson's house. During the hearing, Watson was eventually discharged for lack of any compelling testimony.

To add to the mix of suspects, some researchers are convinced Belle Starr's killer was her own son, Edwin, whom everyone called Eddie. A brooding and sullen youth, Eddie was seventeen years of age at the time and was known to hate his mother. For one thing, Eddie deeply resented Belle's marriage to Jim July. For another, Eddie was jealous of the attention Belle showered on Pearl. Furthermore, Eddie was growing tired of the frequent whippings inflicted on him by his mother, and the two often quarreled violently.

A few days earlier, Eddie had wanted to take his mother's best horse to a dance in a neighboring community. She refused him, but he took it anyway, stayed gone for several days, and returned home drunk and sick. Belle went into a rage when she saw how her favorite horse had been abused. Snatching up a quirt, she whipped Eddie unmercifully.

A few days following the whipping, Eddie, still angry, told several people he was going to kill his mother. Dr. Charles Mooney, who treated Eddie after the whipping, wrote that the youth had told him the same thing.

Belle Starr was buried in the front yard of the cabin at Younger's Bend. A short time later, thieves opened the grave and removed jewelry from the body along with a revolver that was interred with her. Soon afterward, Pearl hired a stonemason to construct a two-foot tall wall of rock around the site and cover it with a limestone roof. The engraving on the tombstone reads:

Shed not for her a bitter tear
Nor give the heart to vain regret;
'Tis but the casket that lies here,
The gem that filled it sparkles yet.

No one was ever convicted of the killing of Belle Starr. While theories abound, the identity of her murderer remains one of the most puzzling mysteries of the Old West.

FOURTEEN

Did Bill Longley Escape the Gallows?

Like the outlaw Bill Smith, Bill Longley never garnered the notoriety and newspaper headlines as did other Western bad men. Nor did Longley inspire the dime novelists to any degree to recreate and fantasize his adventures and outlawry for readers. In spite of the comparative paucity of publicity generated by this hardened killer, fact and lore associated with his exploits combine to suggest he may have killed well over thirty men.

Bill Longley has been described by some writers as a serial killer, an identification that appears to be accurate. Longley's penchant for killing caught up with him, however, when he was captured, tried, convicted, and sentenced to hang in Giddings, Texas, in 1878. Whether or not it was Bill Longley that was hanged, however, remains a mystery. Many are convinced the killer never met his fate on the gallows but was allowed to escape and live out the remainder of his life in Louisiana under the alias of John Calhoun Brown.

Bill Longley was born in 1851. At an early age he demonstrated skill with guns and a propensity for violence. When he was fifteen years old and growing up in Austin County, Texas, he killed his first man, a deed that troubled him not at all and one he never regretted.

The year was 1866, and central Texas, as well as other parts of the South, was recovering from the end of the Civil War and suffering the ongoing processes related to the establishment of Union rule. Austin County, like many other locations in Texas, was filling up with carpetbaggers, Union officials, and Yankee politicians and businessmen, a trend that antagonized the local residents.

With the end of the Civil War, a brand new Texas state police force was created and consisted, in part, of a number of newly freed slaves. Most of them carried out their jobs honorably. A few, imbued with a newfound sense of power and accompanying arrogance, often went out of the way to aggravate Texas's white settlers.

One afternoon as young Bill Longley was walking down the main street of the tiny community of Old Evergreen, he paused to watch a newly arrived black policeman riding through town. As the policeman guided his mount along the narrow road, he loudly cursed the whites that were watching him from the store and staring from the sidewalks. From time to time the policeman raised his rifle and pointed it at one of the townsfolk. One of the white men who received a loud cursing and found himself looking down the barrel of the policeman's rifle was Bill Longley's father.

Confidently, the younger Longley stepped out into the middle of the street, faced the policeman, and told him to put his gun away. Stunned that this youthful intruder would challenge him, the lawman merely stared dumbfounded at the boy. It was his undoing. In a flash, Longley pulled out a pistol and shot the policeman, killing him instantly.

Given the strong anti-Union sentiments at the time, townspeople carried the body of the dead policeman away and buried it in an unmarked grave. Young Longley, rather than being charged with the killing, was thereafter regarded as a hero in the town.

Making a decent living in central Texas during post–Civil War days was difficult for most, but it was especially so for a young man like Longley. He longed for something better than sharecropping or serving as a blacksmith's apprentice. The disenchantment for life in Old Evergreen, accompanied by his growing spirit of adventure, took hold of Bill Longley. One day he rode away to seek his fortune elsewhere.

Life was not much better in other places, at least not at first. During the next few months, Longley drifted from one cow camp to another, from one cornfield to the next. His travels took him to Arkansas, Oklahoma, Kansas, Wyoming, and the Dakotas. The young man soon tired of working the land and turned to other ways of making a living. He discovered gambling and in a short time learned he was good at cards. At one time he operated a saloon in the Black Hills of South Dakota, where he successfully separated newfound gold from the miners at the bar and the gaming tables.

During this time, Bill Longley committed a number of robberies and holdups, and it is certain that he killed several men in the process. Longley was earning a reputation as a man with a fierce temper, and some claimed that he killed mostly during fits of anger. Others have written that he killed for the sheer joy of watching men die. According to some researchers, several of Longley's murders took place in ambushes. In other cases, some of his victims were goaded into fights by the confident and quick-drawing gunman.

On at least one occasion, Longley killed out of paranoia. Once, while working as a cowhand, Longley shot and killed a man who was merely looking at him. He said he couldn't sleep because the cowboy just sat and watched him all the time. One night Longley became so aggravated at being watched that he crawled out of his bedroll, picked up a gun, and shot the man in the head. After holstering his gun, Longley climbed back into his bedroll and fell asleep immediately.

Bloody Bill Longley eventually drifted back to Texas and in 1877 settled in Giddings, where he located some kin. Not long after his arrival, one of his cousins was shot and killed. Longley wasted no time in hunting down the offender and killing him in turn. At the time, Longley claimed it as the thirty-second man he'd killed.

For this deed, however Longley was not treated like the hero he was in 1866 when he killed the policeman. Instead, he was arrested, charged with murder, and sentenced to hang. "Hanging," Longley wrote in a letter to a woman, "is my favorite way of dying." Bill Longley was twenty-seven years old at the time.

The facts surrounding the hanging are confusing and conflicting. At least one account claims Longley was executed in front of "a crowd of 4,000 that had assembled." Another account states that Longley was escorted out of town by the sheriff and a deputy and was allegedly hanged with only the two lawmen present. Still others claim another prisoner, a Longley look-alike, was hanged in the killer's place. The body of the hanged man was buried the same day in the Giddings cemetery.

A short time after the hanging, a story made the rounds in Lee, Burleson, Travis, and Austin Counties that the sheriff who was given the responsibility of carrying out the hanging was bribed by Longley and that the lawman helped the gunman escape to Louisiana. Another tale, this one from Longley kin in Giddings, suggests that Longley and the sheriff were friends and that the lawman aided the outlaw's escape out of loyalty.

Whatever the truth, the body of the man hanged as Bill Longley was carried to the Giddings cemetery and interred. A marker, a piece of petrified wood, was erected over the site.

As time passed, more curious tales about Bill Longley surfaced. One of the most intriguing concerned a Louisiana farmer and businessman who went by the name of John Calhoun Brown. Brown was a somewhat reclusive and mysterious figure and very little is known about him. According to the tales, Brown showed up in a small Louisiana community two weeks after Bill Longley was allegedly hanged. Brown purchased a farm and during the ensuing years made a good living growing cotton. A few central Texas residents who knew Longley and encountered Brown in Louisiana maintained they were the same man. It was also related that members of the Longley family always knew the killer escaped the gallows to live out the remainder of his life in Louisiana. According to research, Calhoun aka Bill Longley died in 1926.

Over the years, a number of researchers began to wonder who was actually buried in the Giddings cemetery—Longley or a substitute. As time passed, the marker identifying the so-called Longley gravesite was accidentally removed and for years no one was ever certain of the exact location.

One of the people interested in whether or not it was Bill Longley that was buried at Giddings was anthropologist Douglas Owlsley. Owlsley, associated with the Smithsonian Institution, was sent to Giddings to try to find some answers.

During the summer of 1998 Owlsley, accompanied by his assistants and using a 1920 photograph of the gravesite, identified what they believed to be the location where the hanged man was buried. After receiving permission from authorities, the scientists dug into the site and found several teeth and some bones. Owlsley stated that the bones belonged to "a tall man who died young." The remains were sent to the University of Texas at San Antonio for study.

It was later determined via DNA testing that the remains belonged to someone who was related to the descendants of the Longley family, and thus a conclusion was formed that the bones were those of outlaw Bill Longley.

The conclusion may have been premature. Some have claimed that the grave that was excavated was not the location where Longley was supposed to have been buried. Others insist that the bones belong to a Longley relative that was interred there. Since a number of Longley's kin have been buried in the Giddings cemetery this is a distinct possibility.

Today, some Longley descendants continue to insist that their famous ancestor did, in fact, flee to Louisiana and lived out the remainder of his life as John Calhoun Brown.

FIFTEEN

◆◆◆

How Did John Wilkes Booth Die?

History records that on the evening of April 14, 1865, the renowned actor John Wilkes Booth shot and killed President Abraham Lincoln as the chief executive watched a play at Ford's Theater in Washington, D.C. There was never any doubt as to the identity of the slayer; dozens who knew Booth and were in attendance witnessed the assassination.

The subsequent nine-day pursuit and so-called capture and killing of John Wilkes Booth, however, remains one of the most controversial, contradictory, and, according to many historians, conspiratorial episodes in American history. As the mysteries surrounding the pursuit of Booth have gradually unraveled during the past century, and as new lost and long-suppressed information has become available, a number of researchers are convinced that Booth was, in fact, never captured or killed. More and more, investigators are growing convinced that the man killed at Richard Henry Garrett's Virginia farm was not Booth at all but a Confederate officer and a victim of mistaken identity.

If true, then what became of John Wilkes Booth? A number of stories have surfaced over the years purporting to explain his fate. Most have Booth living for another twenty years or more beyond the assassination. A variety of evidence has surfaced placing a man who could have been Booth in such diverse places as England, India, Rome, Paris, Vienna, California, Texas, and Oklahoma. While some of this evidence is compelling, it is, nevertheless, not proof. Since the so-called capture and killing of Booth in Virginia, at least twenty-two different men have subsequently been identified as the famous assassin. Most of these men were clearly imposters, some were merely cases of mistake identity, but one or two continue to baffle researchers.

Perhaps one of the most mysterious cases with regard to what actually became of Booth is that associated with a curious man named David E. George, who died in Enid, Oklahoma, in 1903.

John Wilkes Booth.
Source: Library of Congress, Prints & Photographs Division,
LC-DIG-ppmsca-23892

To achieve as complete an understanding of David E. George as possible, one must examine the experience of Finis L. Bates, beginning
with his residence in Granbury, Texas, during the early 1870s. During
this time, Bates was a young lawyer trying to earn a living in this quiet
little town some forty miles southwest of Fort Worth.

One morning a man who called himself John St. Helen stopped
by Bates' office and asked the young lawyer to defend him against a
charge of operating a saloon without a license in the nearby town of
Glen Rose. St. Helen informed Bates that he was, in fact, guilty of the
charge but stated that he would resist appearing at a federal court

hearing in Tyler. The man told Bates his real name was not John St. Helen and that he was deeply concerned his true identity would be discovered. The risk, he told the lawyer, was too great.

Several weeks later, St. Helen moved to Granbury where he began to spend more time with Bates. In a book titled *Escape and Suicide of John Wilkes Booth, Assassin of President Lincoln*, Bates later described St. Helen as having "more money than was warranted by his stock in trade." According to Bates, St. Helen had "penetrating black eyes" that manifested "desperation and a capacity for crime."

Bates also wrote that St. Helen showed an "intimacy with every detail of theatrical work," and kept theater-related periodicals in his room. St. Helen could recite most of Shakespeare's plays and was particularly fond of *Richard III*, known to be the favorite play of John Wilkes Booth.

Late one evening in 1877, Lawyer Bates was summoned to the bedside of St. Helen who was seriously ill. In a weak and halting voice, St. Helen told Bates he did not think he would live much longer. He instructed the lawyer to look under his pillow where he would find a tintype. Bates searched for and found the tintype that bore the image of a somewhat younger John St. Helen.

St. Helen told the lawyer that, should he die, to please send the picture to Edwin Booth in Baltimore with a note explaining that the subject had passed away. Gasping for breath, St. Helen partially rose from the bed, placed a hand on Bates' forearm, and told the lawyer that he was John Wilkes Booth, the assassin of President Lincoln.

Stunned, Bates promised that he would, if necessary, send the tintype to Edwin Booth. Bates sat up with St. Helen throughout the remainder of the night.

St. Helen did not die, but he remained very ill for several weeks. Eventually he began to show improvement. When he was almost completely recovered, he invited Bates to walk with him some distance from town, explaining to the lawyer that he needed to speak about a delicate matter. During the walk, St. Helen once again confessed that he was Booth and pleaded with Bates to keep the knowledge secret. When the lawyer agreed to do so, St. Helen spent the next few hours revealing a number of details regarding the assassination of Abraham Lincoln.

According to St. Helen, wrote Bates, Vice President Andrew Johnson was the principal instigator of the assassination of the president. St. Helen related that he visited with Johnson on the afternoon of

April 14, only hours prior to the killing, and that the vice president informed him that it would be arranged for General Grant to leave town and that the way would be cleared to allow the killer to escape into Maryland.

Throughout the entire conversation that afternoon, St. Helen related pertinent aspects of the murder of Lincoln, the subsequent escape from Ford's Theater, and the flight through the Maryland and Virginia countryside. St. Helen's details and descriptions were remarkable in their depth and intricacy. For his part, Bates respected the confidentiality of St. Helen's admission. Initially, however, he did not believe any of St. Helen's words.

Much of St. Helen's description and information, as it was related to Bates, has been questioned by researchers. Some, however, maintain that the account provided by St. Helen could only have come from someone quite intimate with the facts of the assassination, particularly those associated with the final confrontation at Garrett's farm. Many of the points related by St. Helen were virtually unknown to historians at the time, and some differed markedly from accepted facts.

If St. Helen were merely an imposter, one must wonder why he did not relate what were considered to be well-known and well-publicized aspects of the assassination and flight. Instead, he provided versions somewhat different from the commonly accepted and oft-published ones, versions that, on investigation, bear a provocative level of credibility.

One particularly telling piece of information had to do with Booth's diary. Most historians claim the assassin's diary was taken from the pockets of the dying man at Garrett's farm. According to papers and journals recently analyzed by researchers David Balsiger and Charles E. Sellier, however, Booth's diary was apparently lost in a grove of trees near Gambo Creek in Virginia, a location where he hid with a companion during his escape, and this fact was unknown to most who have studied the assassin's flight. St. Helen told Bates that on April 22, he had "discovered that he had lost [his] diary, some letters, and a picture of my sister."

St. Helen also told Bates that on April 24 he fled westward through West Virginia and Kentucky, eventually making his way to Mississippi and thence into Indian Territory. After spending some time in the American West, St. Helen went into Mexico and disguised himself as a priest. From Mexico he traveled to California in 1866 or 1867 where he met with his mother and his older brother Junius in San Francisco.

Time passed and St. Helens drifted to New Orleans where he spent a year teaching school and going by the alias of Mr. Ney. Following this, he moved to Texas and eventually settled in Glen Rose where he assumed the name John St. Helen and managed a saloon. In 1872 he moved to Granbury.

Several months following St. Helen's revelations, Lawyer Bates moved to Memphis, Tennessee, where he established what eventually became a very successful law practice. In his spare time he began reading everything he could find about the assassination of Abraham Lincoln and the life and times of John Wilkes Booth. The more he studied these subjects, the more he grew convinced that John St. Helen was the man who killed President Lincoln.

On January 13, 1903, the body of a man named David E. George was transported from his room at the Grand Avenue Hotel in Enid, Oklahoma, to the undertaking establishment of W. B. Penniman. George, known around Enid as a handyman and house painter, had committed suicide. George was also known by a few Enid residents as a heavy drinker and many also suspected he was a drug addict since, they claimed, he regularly took morphine. His death, it was subsequently determined, was caused by an ingestion of a large dose of strychnine.

While Penniman's assistant, W. H. Ryan, was embalming George's body, the Reverend E. C. Harper stopped by for a visit. Harper was a Methodist minister, and he had just completed a service in the outer room of the funeral parlor. Harper glanced down at the body of George and cried out, "Do you know who this is?"

When assistant Ryan said he did not, Harper explained that the body belonged to none other that John Wilkes Booth, the assassin of President Abraham Lincoln. He told Ryan that George had confessed his identity to Mrs. Harper three years earlier. Mrs. Harper visited the funeral parlor three days later and identified the corpse of David E. George as the man who admitted to her in El Reno, Oklahoma, in 1900 that he was Booth. She later wrote out and signed a statement attesting to her peculiar experience.

During the next few days, newspapers around the country carried the story that a man believed by some to be Lincoln's assassin had died in Enid. In Memphis, Finis Bates read one such article and wondered if the dead man named David E. George might be the man he once knew as John St. Helen. He decided to go find out for himself.

Bates departed Memphis and arrived in Enid on January 23. On the following morning he went to the undertaker's establishment to view the body. After staring at the corpse for a long time, Bates removed a folder from his valise and from it withdrew the tintype of John St. Helen he still possessed. He held the picture next to the face of the corpse. It was, according to Bates, the same man.

For several days the body remained on display at Pennington's establishment. Because it went unclaimed, it was eventually placed in a back room where it was stored for years. Finally, Bates came forward and took possession of the body.

While investigating aspects of the life of David E. George, Bates learned he had worked as a house painter in El Reno. When he wasn't working, which was most of the time, George apparently hung around a number of retail establishments as well as the police station. Bates also discovered that George regularly received large amounts of money from mysterious sources. Though it was never proven, the lawyer was convinced that George, like St. Helen, was getting money from the Booth family. Bates learned that at his death George was worth approximately $30,000 and carried a $5,000 life insurance policy. In April 1900, George, in a fit of depression, swallowed a large amount of prescription drugs and sincerely believed he was going to die. While still barely conscious, he told a Miss Young, who was soon to become the wife of Reverend Harper, that he had a confession to make. He told her that he had killed "one of the best men whoever lived, Abraham Lincoln." He asked the woman to bring him a pen and paper and when she did he scribbled, "I am going to die before the sun goes down," and signed it "J. Wilkes Booth."

George recovered from this suicide attempt and several weeks later moved to Enid, about sixty-five miles to the north. During the morning of January 13, 1903, while staying at Enid's Grand Avenue Hotel, George swallowed a fatal dose of strychnine and died a short time later.

Were St. Helen and George the same man? And was one or the other or both John Wilkes Booth? This mystery has baffled researchers for over a century. Some critical historians, George S. Bryan foremost among them, contend that Bates worked very hard to make St. Helen and George appear to be the same, and in so doing purposely altered some of the facts. In spite of Bryan's criticisms, St. Helen and George did share a number of characteristics: They drank heavily; they were inclined to be loud and boisterous on occasion; both carried a gun; and both were known to recite extended soliloquies and poetry. Both men were also apparently well educated, and both were quite intimate with the theater, especially Shakespeare. While living in El Reno, George was remembered as having participated in a number of amateur productions and providing some excellent performances.

Both St. Helen and George dressed in the manner of Booth. Bates noted that both men wore "a black semi-dress suit style, of the best fabrics, always with the turndown Byron collar and dark tie . . . tailor made, new and well-pressed, pants well-creased, shoes new patent leather and hat a new black Stetson derby."

George possessed certain physical characteristics that were similar to those of Booth. The only officially recognized comparison study of the day was employed to evaluate the features of both David E. George and John Wilkes Booth and some similarities were found. The shape of George's head, specifically the structure of the forehead, as well as the contour of the face around the eyes and the jaw line, bear a striking resemblance to Booth. The analysis also revealed that the structure of the nose, particularly the bridge, the "indenture of [George's] left nostril, and the distance from nose to mouth bear a strong resemblance to Booth's." Other features described by the analysis included a cocked right eyebrow manifested by both men, the ears, and the striking similarity of the hands.

Skeptics state that the color of George's eyes was enough to dismiss the claim that he was Booth. His eyes, as described by the mortician, were blue-gray. According to a number of government documents, Booth's eyes were black. In contradiction to this information, Asa Booth, the actor's sister, wrote that they were not black but hazel.

George, according to Bates, bore the marks of a broken right leg, not the left that Booth broke at the end of his leap at Ford's Theater. Others who have examined the corpse stated that they found no evidence of a break at all.

George's signature as "J. Wilkes Booth," according to some analysts, bore little resemblance to known samples of Booth's handwriting. Others insist there were certain similarities.

A Dr. Clarence True Wilson was in possession of the George/Booth mummy for three years, during which time he studied it extensively. Wilson told a writer in 1932 that he had conducted a thorough examination of the Booth-George similarities and was convinced they were one and the same.

Bates showed photographs of St. Helen and George to a number of people who had known Booth. The city editor at the El Reno newspaper was a man named Brown who had lived in Washington, D.C., Baltimore, and New York during the 1860s, regularly attended the theater, and saw Booth perform many times. On being shown photographs of George, Brown stated, "I never saw David E. George, but these are pictures of John Wilkes Booth."

Brown, who was serving in the army at the time of the assassination, was in Washington when the body of the man killed at Garrett's farm arrived. He told Bates that "there was a belief, quite general among members of the federal army with whom I came in contact, that the body . . . was not that of John Wilkes Booth."

Bates also showed photographs of Booth to L. Threadkell who once employed St. Helen as a teamster in 1867. Threadkell unhesitatingly identified the images of Booth as John St. Helen.

Joseph Jefferson was a childhood friend of Booth's and a fellow actor, having performed alongside the famous thespian a number of times on the stage. When Bates showed him the tintype of St. Helen and photographs of George, Jefferson, after studying them closely for a time, said, "This is John Wilkes Booth."

Another stunning piece of evidence relates to a signet ring worn by Booth. The actor was seldom seen without the ring that bore his initials and had been photographed numerous times while wearing it. The ring, prized by the assassin, was not on the finger of the man killed at Garrett's farm.

David E. George wore a similar ring. Some weeks before he died from the dose of strychnine, George told a neighbor that he was being followed. One afternoon, on spotting the approach of two law enforcement authorities, George was in fear that he would be identified. He removed the telltale ring from his finger and swallowed it.

In December 1931, the mummy of George was examined by a group of seven physicians at Chicago's Northwestern University. The group was headed by Dr. Otto L. Schmidt, former president of the prestigious Chicago Historical Society. Another member of the examining team was Dr. Lewis L. McArthur, one of the country's leading X-ray specialists at the time.

The George mummy was subjected to X-rays and dissection. During the examination, according to the report, the team found evidence of a broken leg, although it was not stated whether it was the left or right.

The most astounding discovery, however, was that of a ring that somehow became embedded in the flesh of the body cavity. Though the surface had been modified somewhat as the apparent result of the action of digestive juices over time, it was believed the initials "JWB" could be discerned on its face. Dr. Schmidt subsequently wrote, "I can say safely that we believe Booth's body is here in my office."

The evidence for St. Helen being George and for either or both being John Wilkes Booth remains provocative, yet inconclusive. A number of researchers are convinced that George was, in fact, the assassin Booth. Many of those discrediting the George mummy as being that of Booth have been journalists and, as author Theodore Roscoe says, journalists are not professional detectives.

The mystery persists.

The fate of the David E. George mummy presents yet another mystery. At one point, Bates tried to sell it to the *Dearborn Independent* for $10,000. Another time he offered it to Henry Ford. Both declined to purchase it. During the 1920s and 1930s, Bates leased the mummified corpse to a carnival promoter who charged patrons twenty-five cents to view "The Assassin of President Abraham Lincoln." The body was still being displayed in the 1940s, but a short time later the promoter went bankrupt and moved to Declo, Idaho, where he placed the mummy in a chair and charged neighbors ten cents to view it. The mummy eventually disappeared, and to this day no one is certain of its whereabouts. It is reputed to exist in a private collection somewhere.

In 1990, three research pathologists at the Regional Forensic Center in Memphis, Tennessee, undertook a search for the long-lost mummy. They were convinced that David E. George was John Wilkes Booth and they believed they could prove it if they could only find the mummy and examine it. To date, the mummy has not been located and the search continues.

SIXTEEN

The Killing of John Wesley Hardin

John Wesley Hardin may have been the deadliest gunfighter the Old West ever knew. He certainly was if you believe his own accounts of his numerous killings, accounts that he related in his autobiography, *The Life of John Wesley Hardin.* Even discounting Hardin's braggadocio and exaggerations, and in spite of some of his harshest critics, he still emerges as one of the most dangerous gunmen the West has ever seen, perhaps the worst ever. At least one writer has referred to Hardin as a "psychopathic" killer.

Hardin's death, like his life, was full of contradiction and mystery, and very few people, ranging from eyewitnesses to intrepid researchers, can agree on what actually happened. Why he was killed and the manner in which his death occurred are still discussed and debated today.

John Wesley Hardin was born in Bonham, Texas, fifteen miles south of the Oklahoma border on May 26, 1853. He was named after the founder of the Methodist faith by his father, himself a Methodist minister. When Hardin was fifteen years old, according to one story, he killed his first man, a former slave who refused to grant him right-of-way on a narrow road. While neighbors in Bonham could find little fault with Hardin's act, a trio of Reconstructionist troops was sent to arrest the killer. Waiting in ambush, Hardin shot all three down using a shotgun and a revolver.

Not wishing to remain in the area as a fugitive, Hardin fled into East Texas, where he lived for several years. While there, according to his own words, he killed several more men.

Hardin's path eventually took him to Oklahoma on a trail drive, during which he claimed to have killed another seven men. In Abilene, Kansas, he allegedly backed down the famous Wild Bill Hickok and shortly afterward killed two more men. More time passed and he decided to return to Texas. In between more killings in Texas, Hardin managed to find time to marry June Bowen, who subsequently gave him two daughters and a son.

In 1872 Hardin was arrested and placed in the jail in Gonzales, Texas. A few days later a friend smuggled him a saw and he escaped, fleeing once again deep into East Texas, where he became a participant in the famous and violent Sutton-Taylor Feud. Siding with the Taylors, Hardin's guns soon claimed more victims, including at least two deputy sheriffs.

The second deputy was killed on Hardin's twenty-first birthday. Charles Webb, a Brown County deputy sheriff, arrived in Comanche where Hardin was living at the time. According to one story, Webb claimed he was only in town to visit relatives. Hardin, however, was convinced the lawman was there to kill him. The two men encountered one another in a Comanche saloon, spoke briefly, and even shook hands. When Hardin turned away from Webb and walked toward the bar, the deputy allegedly drew his revolver. Reacting swiftly to a shouted warning, Hardin turned while drawing his own gun and fired at Webb, the bullet striking him in the head.

Hardin fled once again, this time traveling to Alabama, Georgia, and Florida, and going by the alias J. H. Swain. Shortly after his departure, a revenge-minded mob caught up with Hardin's brother Joe and hung him. A short time later, the state of Texas posted a $4,000 reward for the capture of John Wesley Hardin.

Weeks later, Texas Rangers caught up with Hardin and a friend aboard a train near Pensacola, Florida. The companion decided to fight it out with the lawmen and reached for his gun. For his effort he was shot down. At that point, Hardin stepped into the aisle of the passenger car and began yelling that he was being robbed. He attempted to pull his own revolver to put up a defense, but the hammer became snagged in his suspenders. While Hardin tried to free the gun, one of the Rangers knocked him unconscious with the butt of a rifle and placed him in custody.

Hardin was brought into court, tried, and found guilty of killing Charles Webb. The judge sentenced him to twenty-five years in the state prison at Huntsville.

The prisoner Hardin metamorphosed into a remarkably different individual from the gunman Hardin. Shortly after his incarceration, Hardin began reading everything available, with most of his efforts directed toward the Bible and law books. In time he was teaching Sunday school and leading the prison debate team. He also began writing his biography.

For a while Hardin was convinced he wanted to become a minister on his release, but he eventually abandoned that plan in favor of practicing law. More than anything, according to a letter he wrote home, Hardin was anxious to be reunited with his family.

It was not to happen. While he was in prison, Hardin's wife died, an event that had a telling effect on the man many consider to be the West's deadliest killer.

After serving fifteen years of his sentence, Hardin was released during the winter of 1894. One month later the governor of Texas granted him a full pardon. Hardin moved back to Gonzales, and the former prisoner became certified to practice law and soon became involved in local politics.

Growing frustrated at the strange machinations of the political world, Hardin did not remain long in Gonzales. He moved to Junction where he spent as much or more time playing cards as practicing law. During one card game, Hardin won a fourteen-year-old girl from her father. Drunk, Hardin married the girl but abandoned her and the town of Junction and headed for El Paso where he hoped to set up a thriving law practice. Success as a lawyer in El Paso never materialized and, as he did in Junction, Hardin spent most of his time drinking and gambling.

One day a woman named Beulah M'Rose (also spelled Mroz) walked into Hardin's law office and asked him to represent her husband, Martin, on a cattle rustling charge. Badly in need of income, Hardin accepted the case and in no time at all, according to Hardin biographers, he began having an affair with Beulah, a former prostitute. In the meantime, husband Martin waited anxiously across the Rio Grande in Juarez, Mexico.

When Martin M'Rose learned Hardin was carrying on with his wife, he summoned two friends from Eddy County, New Mexico. M'Rose apparently wanted his companions, Tom Finnessy and a man named Lightfoot, to put some pressure on Hardin. The two wrote the gunman-turned-lawyer threatening letters and dared him to come to Juarez. One afternoon in April 1895 Hardin, in the company of El Paso police chief Jeff Milton and U.S. Deputy Marshal George Scarborough, crossed the river to visit a saloon in Juarez. Almost at once they encountered Finnessy and Lightfoot. During an ensuing argument, Hardin punched Lightfoot who stumbled backward against a wall. Hardin drew a revolver from his waistband and jammed it into his adversary's stomach. When Milton interfered, Hardin turned his attention to Finnessy and cracked him hard in the jaw with his closed fist. If was clear Hardin had lost neither his courage nor his enthusiasm for a good fight.

Hardin apparently decided he wanted Martin M'Rose dead, but in uncharacteristic fashion he refrained from going after him personally. Instead, he allegedly hired Milton, Scarborough, Texas Ranger Frank McMahan, and John Selman for the deed. Selman, like Hardin, once had a reputation as a deadly gunfighter and was currently serving as an El Paso constable. With M'Rose dead, said Hardin, the five men would split the $1,000 reward offered for the rustler, as well as whatever money they found in his pockets. In June, using Beulah as bait, M'Rose was lured across the bridge to El Paso and shot dead.

For reasons known only to Hardin, he began drinking more than ever following the killing of M'Rose. He was also growing more and more belligerent, often losing his temper and threatening fellow card players. He even threatened to kill Beulah, who was now living with him.

At one point during the relationship, Beulah was arrested for drunkenness by John Selman Jr., an El Paso police officer. On the afternoon of August 19, Hardin entered into a heated argument with the elder Selman. Some claim the argument was over Beulah's arrest by Selman's son, but others maintain the two men quarreled because John Selman demanded money he thought he was due for helping to kill M'Rose.

That same evening, Hardin went to the Acme Saloon and, while drinking at the bar, started gambling with El Paso businessman Henry Brown. The two were playing a dice game called Ship, Captain, and Crew, and during his turn, Hardin shook the dice and tossed them out onto the bar. After examining the lay of the dice, he looked up at Brown and informed him he had four sixes to beat.

According to witnesses, those were John Wesley Hardin's last words. No sooner had he spoken them than John Selman burst through the door of the saloon and shot Hardin three times, killing him instantly. Hardin was forty-two years old.

The reason for the killing and the manner in which it occurred has remained a mystery for well over a century.

Motive is one element of the killing of John Wesley Hardin that is yet to be determined. Over and over, researchers have failed to come to any agreement over John Selman's reason for killing Hardin. The truth is, he may have had several. Selman himself claimed he shot Hardin in order to keep his son safe. He believed, according to some, that following the arrest of Beulah, Hardin had threatened John Selman Jr. In killing Hardin, the elder Selman was convinced he was only protecting a member of his family.

Some have speculated that Selman killed Hardin because he was bitter that he was not included in the division of the money taken from the body of Martin M'Rose. According to author Leon Metz, Selman approached businessman George Look and complained to him that Hardin gave him none of the money. Selman implied to Look that he might kill Hardin. It has also been reported that Selman felt threatened by Hardin. Selman was heard stating that he believed Hardin wanted to kill him.

Elsewhere, Metz has suggested Selman's motive may simply have been jealousy, that "Selman might have shot Hardin to keep himself center-stage among gunmen." While there is the possibility of a grain of truth to that observation, most scholars do not take it seriously.

As for the actual killing, Selman himself testified that he stepped into the Acme Saloon, confronted Hardin face-to-face, and shot him dead. After Hardin fell to the floor, Selman shot him twice more, once in the chest near the right nipple and once near the right shoulder. There were at least a dozen witnesses in the Acme Saloon at the time who observed the killing, so it would seem that the truth of what happened could easily have been determined. Unfortunately, that was not the case. In fact, the versions given by the witnesses offered considerable variation and contradiction.

Shorty Anderson, seated at the rear of the saloon, was watching Hardin and Brown play dice. Anderson claimed he saw Hardin react to Selman's shout, turn, and reach for a pistol just before he was shot. Policeman Frank Carr, after examining Hardin's body stated that the victim's pistol had gotten caught in the tight waistband of the pants, reminiscent of Hardin's attempt to defend himself while being arrested in Florida years earlier.

A man named Brock examined the wound closely and offered the opinion that the bullet had entered the right eye and come out the back of the head. Brock, however, was a cattle buyer, not a physician.

The Acme bartender, Frank Patterson, saw it differently. He stated in court that Hardin, standing at the bar, had his back to the front door of the saloon when Selman walked in. According to Patterson, Selman shouted something at Hardin. Before Hardin could turn, Selman leveled his revolver within two feet of the back of his head and shot him.

Henry Brown, the man playing Ship, Captain, and Crew with Hardin at the time of the killing, was standing next to the victim when he was killed. Brown, like Patterson, stated that the former gunman's back was turned toward Selman.

The majority of witnesses to the shooting claimed Selman shot Hardin in the back of the head. Three physicians who examined the wound concurred that the bullet "entered the back of the skull and came out of the left eye." County Attorney D. Storms also provided the opinion that the victim was shot in the back of the head.

Ultimately Selman was acquitted and a new trial was scheduled for several months later. He was destined never to appear. On April 2, 1896, an Easter Sunday, Selman spent much of the day drinking in El Paso's Wigwam Saloon. Well after midnight a very drunk Selman left to go home and on the way encountered George Scarborough. An argument ensued and guns were drawn and fired. Selman died later that afternoon with four of Scarborough's bullets in his body.

Was John Wesley Hardin shot in the back of the head by John Selman? Or was the former gunman facing his killer? Why the confusion among eyewitnesses over what happened? No one seems to know for certain.

SEVENTEEN

The Strange Tale of Black Bart, the Poet-Robber of California

One of the most unusual, unorthodox, and mysterious bandits in American history was Charles E. Boles, better known as Black Bart. During his career in outlawry, Boles is believed to have committed twenty-eight robberies, almost entirely of Wells Fargo and Company stagecoaches. Boles is regarded as California's most successful bandit, high praise indeed for an outlaw when one considers the number of noted desperadoes who roamed the Golden State.

For his crimes, Black Bart was eventually captured, tried, convicted, and sentenced to six years in the California State Prison at San Quentin. Soon after he was released in 1888, Boles, according to a number of historians, immediately returned to robbing Wells Fargo stagecoaches.

By the time 1888 drew to a close, Charles E. Boles, despite the efforts of Wells Fargo authorities to track him, simply disappeared. According to most researchers, he was never seen again. While a variety of rumors relative to his fate circulated throughout California, no one, not even his family, ever knew what happened to him. What became of Charles Boles, aka Charles E. Bowles, aka Black Bart, remains a mystery to this day.

According to biographer Laika Dajani, Charles E. Boles was born in Norfolk County, England, in 1829. At the time, the family name was Bowles, and it is believed that Charles changed the spelling of his surname to Boles when he became an adult. When Charles was only one year old, his family immigrated to Jefferson County, New York, where the elder Bowles farmed and eventually raised ten children.

Young Charley, as he was called, was a stout boy possessed of "uncommon strength and endurance," characteristics that perhaps assisted him in surviving a childhood bout of smallpox.

When he was twenty years old, Charley was carried along in the wave of interest and excitement over the fabulous gold discoveries in Northern California. Newspaper stories and accounts of some of the gold seekers returning home fired his enthusiasm for wealth and adventure. Along with his brother David, Boles traveled west to seek his fortune. On arriving in California, the brothers found the work hard and the competition fierce, and after two years of limited success and going hungry, they returned home, broke.

Charley was not discouraged, however. After remaining in New York for a few weeks he organized another trip to California. Once again David accompanied him, as did another brother, Robert. This venture proved costly—David and Robert took sick shortly after their arrival in California and died. After burying his brothers, Charley returned to New York, remained a short time, and headed west once again.

Charley ran out of money in Illinois and took a job farming. Here he met and married Mary Elizabeth Johnson, probably in 1856, and sired four children. Life for him was good in Illinois, and for a time the gold fever that initially attracted him to California subsided.

When the Civil War broke out, Boles enlisted in the Union army. Following the war he retuned to the Illinois farm but now found little satisfaction in tilling, planting, and harvesting. Dreams of riches crowded his thoughts, and California was luring him once again. Boles was convinced he could make a fortune in the gold mines this time, so he filled a pack, said goodbye to his family, and headed west.

Boles traveled to Montana where he filed a claim on a small but profitable gold mine. He worked many long hours alone on the mine extracting the ore and making a decent living. He regularly sent money to his family in Illinois.

One day while he was working at his mine, Boles was approached by representatives of Wells Fargo who told him they were interested in purchasing his holdings. Over a period of several weeks, Wells Fargo agents made Boles a number of offers for his mine, but he refused to sell. So eager was the express company to gain Boles's claim that they conspired to divert his water supply, ultimately forcing him to abandon the area. When Boles moved out, Wells Fargo moved in. The event marked the beginning of perspectives that were to thereafter shape the future of Charles Boles. He grew bitter and harbored an intense hatred for the Wells Fargo Company. He also became an outlaw.

Weeks later Boles moved to San Francisco where he changed his name to Charles E. Bolton. Bolton cut a dashing figure in the booming city by the bay and identified himself as a businessman who owned several gold mines. His appearance was always neat, and he was described as "well dressed," "quiet," "polite," "gentlemanly," and "fine looking." Bolton was well spoken, not given to profanity, and dined at the finest restaurants. He always carried a cane and wore a derby hat. A short time after Boles, aka Bolton, arrived in San Francisco, Black Bart committed his first robbery.

Around dawn on the morning of July 26, 1875, a passenger-filled Wells Fargo stagecoach was traveling near Copperopolis and was about four miles from its destination at the town of Milton. Suddenly a man stepped out into the road and pointed a double-barreled shotgun at the driver, forcing him to stop the coach. Passengers staring out of the window of the stage saw a figure wearing a flour sack over his head with eyeholes cut into it. The figure was dressed in a derby hat, a short linen coat, and light-colored wool pants. Pointing the gun directly at driver John H. Shine, the highwayman instructed him to drop the express box to the ground. This done, the robber picked up the box and, without saying a word, ran into the nearby woods. Once out of sight of the stage, the bandit chopped the lock away with an axe and retrieved the contents. This first robbery netted Boles a total of $160.

More robberies followed, and a pattern became established: A lone, nattily dressed gunman wearing a flour sack mask appears in the road, stops and robs the stagecoach, grabs the strongbox, and walks away.

The fourth robbery offered a different and intriguing element. After relieving Wells Fargo of $605, the robber left behind a poem hastily scribbled on the back of a waybill:

> I've labored long and hard for bread
> For honor and riches
> But on my corns too long you've tread
> You fine-haired Sons of Bitches
> —Black Bart, the PO8

Now the stagecoach-robbing bandit had a name. Newspapers were carrying stories about Black Bart who, surprisingly to readers and law enforcement authorities, made his escapes on foot.

Black Bart went on to complete a total of twenty-eight robberies over a period of six years. The modus operandi was essentially the same for each. He was well dressed, always masked, generally carried a shotgun along with an axe with which to break open the strongboxes, and Wells Fargo coaches were his favorite targets. At no time was Black Bart ever known to use a horse, and detectives were amazed at the bandit's ability to flee on foot, sometimes covering dozens of miles of rugged California mountain terrain. Furthermore, Black Bart never shot or harmed anyone during any of his robberies.

Black Bart's final robbery before being captured was a repeat of his first years earlier—the Milton stage near Copperopolis. This particular robbery, however, did not transpire as smoothly as the other. Black Bart appeared nervous and clumsy, and as he stuffed money into a sack he carried, the stagecoach guard managed to obtain a gun and sneak up on the bandit. As Black Bart fled from the scene, he dropped a number of items, including his handkerchief.

Within a short time the robbery was reported and detectives arrived at the site of the holdup. The handkerchief was recovered and found to possess a laundry mark—F.X.0.7. It was a simple task for Wells Fargo detective Harry Morse to track down the San Francisco laundry using that mark and identify the customer—C. E. Bolton. A few days later, Morse arrested Boles near the latter's residence on Second Street.

According to Morse, who had staked out the residence, "Bolton," identified by the laundryman as a mine owner, was spotted approaching the house "elegantly dressed and . . . carrying a cane," and wearing a derby hat, a diamond pin, a large diamond ring on his little finger, and a heavy gold watch and chain. Boles, according to Morse, was about five-feet-eight-inches tall, straight as an arrow, broad shoulders, possessed of high cheek bones, deep sunken bright blue eyes, and a large handsome gray mustache.

Morse arranged for an associate to introduce him to Boles. The associate identified Morse as a businessman with an interest in mining. Somehow Morse managed to convince Boles to meet him in the office of Wells Fargo. There, Boles was informed he was under suspicion for robbery and escorted to his hotel room, which was searched. During the process, detectives found several pieces of incriminating evidence.

At his trial, which took place at the Calaveras County Courthouse, Boles remained polite and dignified but denied that he was Black Bart, stating that the robbery for which he was arrested was his first. He eventually pleaded guilty to this robbery of the Milton stagecoach and was sentenced to six years imprisonment at San Quentin.

There was not enough evidence to try Boles on any of the other twenty-seven robberies. Though no record exists, it has been often rumored that, after being sentenced, Boles finally admitted to the other holdups.

Despite the revelation that Black Bart's real name was Charles E. Boles, he was admitted to prison under the name C. E. Bolton, the alias he most often used while in San Francisco. In confinement, Boles was regarded as a model prisoner and undertook his various assignments with enthusiasm and humor. For reasons not known, Boles, who had not communicated with his family in Illinois for twelve years, began writing letters to them following his incarceration.

Boles served only a total of four years and two months before being released on January 21, 1888. He was fifty-nine years old. His release was covered by a few California newspapers, which quoted Boles as saying he hoped to be reunited with his family.

In spite of his stated desire, Boles moved back to San Francisco where, unknown to him at first, he was closely watched by Wells Fargo chief detective Hume and several of his associates.

Approximately one month after his release, Boles traveled south to Visalia. He was followed by two detectives. Once in Visalia, he checked into a hotel using the name Moore. On February 28, 1888, he left town, somehow managing to elude his trackers. When the detectives searched Boles's hotel room they discovered a valise he left behind. When detective Hume examined the contents of the case, he found some clothing items that bore the laundry mark F.X.0.7. Many believe Boles purposely left the items to aggravate the detectives he knew were following him. When Boles left Visalia, it was the last time anyone ever saw him.

Following Boles's disappearance a number of rumors surfaced. Foremost among them was that Wells Fargo offered him a modest pension if he would leave their stagecoaches alone, although no evidence exists relative to this alleged deal. It was also rumored that Boles returned to Illinois and rejoined his family. This, too, is unsubstantiated.

Much to the dismay of Wells Fargo officials, three of its stagecoaches were robbed, with over $4,000 taken. Each of the robberies was conducted in the same fashion as the twenty-eight attributed to Black Bart.

Detective Hume was convinced Boles was the perpetrator of the most recent robberies, but evidence was lacking. Hume alerted Wells Fargo employees and a description of Black Bart was circulated to the various offices. Hume was somehow convinced that Boles was living outside the state and returning from time to time for the express purpose of robbing the coaches. On November 20, 1888, Hume en-listed the help of noted detective W. P. Thomas to track Boles, but the ex-convict was never found.

What happened to Charles Boles? No one knows for certain, but a number of stories circulated for years. Detective Hume was cer-tain Boles left California after disappearing from the Visalia Hotel. He suspected, based on evidence he found, that Boles had moved to Colorado, perhaps Denver. On at least three occasions, Hume was convinced, Boles returned to California to rob Wells Fargo coaches.

Some claimed they encountered Boles in Los Angeles. Others in-sisted he fled to Australia, China, or Mexico. Wells Fargo detectives alternately believed Boles moved to Idaho, Montana, or Utah. Other officers maintained they tracked Boles to Vancouver, British Colum-bia, where he boarded a ship for Japan. John N. Thacker, special of-ficer for Wells Fargo and Company, was convinced Boles eventually settled in Japan.

Another rumor claims Boles was found dead in San Francisco's Commercial Hotel in 1889. Boles's wife, Mary, died in 1896 in Salt Lake City. On her death certificate she is listed as a widow, and some claim she was entirely aware that Boles had passed away.

Several residents of Knights Landing, a small community located some twenty miles northwest of Sacramento, claim Boles quietly moved to that town following his flight from Visalia. They also claim he is buried there in a family plot.

One of the most curious stories relative to what may have happened to Black Bart came from a man named Charles Quedens, who worked as a mail clerk for a San Francisco business establishment. One day in 1903, Quedens related, he was staring out of his office window when he saw a stoutly built old man with a long gray mustache standing guard next to a Wells Fargo express truck. When he asked someone about the identity of the old man he was told it was Black Bart. It was explained to Quedens that the express company hired the former ban-dit as a guard in order to keep him from preying on their stagecoaches. Disbelieving, Quedens introduced himself to the old man and asked him if he was Black Bart. According to Quedens's story, the guard admitted that he was, in fact, the famous outlaw.

No one knows which of these several stories of the fate of Charles Boles contains any truth. George Dane, a descendant of Boles, believes Black Bart, following his release from prison, sent money home to his family and made certain they were financially comfortable. Dane is convinced Boles disappeared from society in order to protect his loved ones from unnecessary notoriety.

For years after his disappearance, Boles's relatives undertook long and arduous searches for him but never encountered a scintilla of information pertinent to his fate. The disappearance of Charles E. Boles, aka Black Bart, will likely never be solved.

EIGHTEEN

✦✦✦

The Return of the Outlaw Butch Cassidy

Thanks to movies, books, magazine articles, and television specials, the outlaw Butch Cassidy has become one of the most widely known and popular outlaw figures of the American West. Accompanied by his friend, Henry Alonzo Longabaugh, aka the Sundance Kid, as well as other members of the notorious gang known as the Wild Bunch, the intriguing Cassidy pursued a successful career robbing trains, banks, and mining camp payrolls.

With lawmen eventually closing in on him, Cassidy fled to South America, joined by Longabaugh and his love interest, the mysterious Etta Place. For a time they farmed and ranched, but Cassidy and Longabaugh soon returned to their outlaw ways of robbing banks and payroll wagons.

Popular and romantic accounts have Cassidy and the Sundance Kid dying in a dramatic shootout with Bolivian soldiers in a small South American village, but reports of this so-called battle are regarded by most serious scholars as unreliable. Whatever the case, the outlaw was never heard from again. At least not in South America.

Several years later, however, a man showed up at many of the Cassidy haunts in North America, a man old friends and relatives maintain was the famous outlaw.

Was Butch Cassidy killed in Bolivia? Or did he survive to return to the United States and visit his family and friends? This mystery has perplexed researchers for decades and continues today.

Butch Cassidy was born Robert Leroy Parker in Beaver, Utah, in 1866. His parents, Max and Annie Parker, migrated years earlier from England in response to Brigham Young's advertisements for settlers and laborers to move to the new Mormon communities that were springing up in Utah. Max and Annie converted to the Mormon faith and eventually relocated the family to Circleville, Utah, where they

Robert LeRoy Parker, aka Butch Cassidy.
Source: Library of Congress, Prints & Photographs Division,
LC-DIG-ppmsca-10772

operated a small ranch. There, young Robert began to manifest skills
as a horseman.

Robert Leroy Parker was charming, mischievous, fun loving, and
possessed of a fine sense of humor. According to all descriptions, he
apparently remained so for the rest of his life. Photographs of the
outlaw generally reveal a certain mischievous gleam in his eye.

When he was a teenager, Parker began using the name Cassidy. Mike
Cassidy was a sometime outlaw of the day and region who somehow

Harry Longabaugh, alias the Sundance Kid, a member of the Wild Bunch.
Source: Library of Congress, Prints & Photographs Division

gained the admiration and respect of the young Parker. The two eventually became close friends. In time, Mike Cassidy instructed Parker in shooting a gun as well as in the rudiments of horse and cattle rustling.

Parker gradually drifted from the family fold and the Mormon faith around 1886 and began running full-time with Mike Cassidy's outlaw gang. After serving what amounts to an apprenticeship, consisting of robbing banks and trains, young Parker eventually formed his own gang. In 1889, along with outlaw companions Tom McCarty and Matt Warner, he robbed a bank in Telluride, Colorado, of over $20,000. After becoming a wanted fugitive, Parker and his followers began hiding out in Brown's Park where he came in contact with other outlaws, such as Elzy Lay, Harvey "Kid Curry" Logan, Ben Kilpatrick, and Will Carver. Known variously as the Wild Bunch and the Hole-in-the-Wall Gang, Parker and his companions roamed outward from Brown's Park to rob banks, trains, and mining company payrolls. In between robberies and rustlings, he worked on ranches in the area, demonstrating superb skills as a breaker and trainer of horses.

For a period of time, Parker, now going by the name George Cassidy, lived in Rock Springs, Wyoming, where he worked as a butcher. As a result of his job, residents started calling him "Butch," and the nickname stuck. Butch Cassidy was eventually arrested for stealing a horse. He was charged, convicted, and in 1894 sentenced to a two-year term at the Wyoming Territorial Prison at Laramie. Whatever form of punishment was intended by the state of Wyoming, it made very little impression on outlaw Cassidy. Released in 1896 after serving one-and-a-half years, he returned to Brown's Park, formed another gang, and went back to robbing banks and trains and stealing horses and cattle.

Cassidy was quite different from most noted outlaws. Though he carried guns and used them on occasion, he never shot a man. In demeanor, he was always charming and affable, easy to get along with, and considerate of others. Cassidy was never known to use foul language.

One of the Wild Bunch's most famous robberies was that of the Union Pacific's Overland Limited near Wilcox, Wyoming. On June 2, 1899, the train was flagged down by one of the gang members. Beneath the express car, a huge charge of dynamite was set off which blew open the door and completely destroyed the vehicle. Once they were inside, a second dynamite charge blew open the safe containing approximately $30,000. After gathering up the loot, the Wild Bunch rode away, escaping easily into the sparsely populated countryside. Their confidence bolstered by this success, the gang went on to rob three more trains over the next several weeks.

Union Pacific officials were growing more and more frustrated with the depredations of Cassidy and the Wild Bunch. The Pinkerton Detective Agency was eventually employed to put an end to the train robberies, but they enjoyed little success. At one point it was reported that Cassidy approached Union Pacific officials about providing amnesty if he promised never to rob another one of their trains. Company officials agreed not to prosecute Cassidy and were reportedly prepared to offer him a job as a payroll guard. Union Pacific representatives and Cassidy arranged a meeting wherein details were to be worked out, but the railroad company officials failed to show up. Cassidy, angered, responded by robbing another train, this time riding away with $55,000.

The railroad company decided it was time to take drastic action. Union Pacific formed a small private army to pursue and capture or kill the outlaws who comprised the Wild Bunch. A company consisting of seasoned ex-lawmen possessing a variety of skills related to crime detection, firearms, and tracking was outfitted and sent in pursuit of the bandits. These railroad mercenaries never caught up with Cassidy and his cohorts, but they came close enough so many times that several potential robberies were foiled.

Realizing that it was only a matter of time before he and members of his gang were caught or killed by lawmen, Cassidy decided it was time to leave the country. With the Sundance Kid and Etta Place, he traveled to New York via Texas in 1901. After spending time and money enjoying the sights and pleasures of New York, the three boarded a ship, the S.S. *Herminius*, and sailed to South America.

After landing in Buenos Aires, Argentina, the fugitives secured a homestead near the small town of Cholila, located near the Chilean border. Cassidy began using the alias James "Santiago" Ryan, and Longabaugh alternately went by the names Harry Place, Harry A. Brown, and Frank Boyd. Cattle, sheep, and horse ranching occupied their time and interest for a while, but some researchers suspect such activity eventually grew boring to the colorful outlaws.

In 1903, the Pinkertons received a tip that Cassidy and Longabaugh were in Argentina, and they sent agent Frank Dimaio to find out if it was true. Dimaio was never able to catch up to the two Americans, but he accumulated abundant evidence of their residence and, prior to returning to the United States, provided Argentine police with wanted posters. At one point during their Argentine residence, Longabaugh and Etta Place returned to the United States for a period of time and then came back.

By 1904, Cassidy learned that Pinkerton detectives were still interested in him and had sent operatives to South America to find him.

He also learned that a reward was still being offered for his capture. During this time, a number of American outlaws fled to South America and took up residence in Argentina or Bolivia. Several of them continued to pursue their outlaw activities in their new homeland, and some historians suspect several robberies attributed to Butch and Sundance were actually committed by others, among them Harvey "Kid Curry" Logan.

In 1906, according to some researchers, Etta Place became very ill and sailed back to the United States, this time apparently for good. Butch and Sundance eventually abandoned their ranch and returned to their outlaw ways. Traveling through parts of Argentina, Bolivia, and Chile, the pair robbed banks and payroll wagons.

Early in 1908 a large payroll being delivered to the Aramayo mines near Quechisla was robbed. Some historians maintain Cassidy and Longabaugh were the perpetrators, taking approximately 80,000 pesos and one mule.

On November 6, the two Americans, both riding mules, entered the Indian village of San Vicente in southern Bolivia. They unloaded the mules and stacked their belongings in a small room adjacent to the home of Bonifacio Casasolo, a town official, and went to look for something to eat.

Around the time the two American strangers returned to the room, a San Vicente policeman recognized one of the newcomer's mules as belonging to a friend who often worked as an escort for the Aramayo mines payroll delivery. The policeman summoned a contingent of Bolivian cavalrymen camped just outside of town. In a short time the room was surrounded. The captain of police approached the building with drawn revolver and instructed the occupants to surrender. A moment later, according to one version of the tale, one of the Americans drew his own weapon and shot one of the soldiers in the neck. The soldier died moments later.

Cavalrymen swarmed into the courtyard as the two Americans kept up a steady stream of gunfire from the doors and windows, and several soldiers were killed in the first rush. During the battle, a man some believe to be the Sundance Kid ran from the room into the courtyard in an attempt to retrieve rifles the two had left there earlier. Halfway to the weapons he was struck several times by bullets and fell to the ground, bleeding. Without hesitating, the second man dashed from the room to his friend and, with bullets kicking up dust around his feet and ricocheting off the walls of the building, dragged him back inside.

The gun battle eventually slowed to sporadic shooting with extended lulls in firing that lasted up to twenty minutes. Around 10:00 PM the soldiers heard two shots from the building, then more silence. The cavalrymen fired occasionally at the structure throughout the night and the next morning, but no more was heard from the Americans. Around noon several soldiers rushed into the room only to find the two strangers dead. They judged that one of the outlaws killed the other. The one who was badly wounded in the courtyard was killed with a bullet to the forehead. The other, it was assumed, turned the gun on himself. The two men were buried that same afternoon at the local cemetery. Union Pacific officials, along with Pinkerton detectives, now rested easy on receiving news that Butch Cassidy was dead.

But was he?

Weeks later, on learning of the deaths of Butch Cassidy and the Sundance Kid, several of the outlaws' friends regarded it as only a rumor, and likely one that was concocted by Cassidy himself. As time passed and no further word was received, people grew more concerned about Butch's fate and desired to learn the truth. Several former companions, led by Matt Warner, took up a collection and sent a representative to South America to ascertain the truth, to find out what exactly happened to Cassidy and Longabaugh.

The representative arrived in San Vicente, interviewed several of the policemen and soldiers involved in the shootout, and returned with photographs of the two dead Americans. The photographs were shown to Cassidy's friend Dr. J. W. K. Bracken. After closely examining the pictures, Bracken stated that one of the men appeared to be the Sundance Kid, but that the other man some thought was Butch Cassidy was Tom Dilley, a Wyoming outlaw who had fled to South America.

As more and more people investigated the San Vicente shootout, the more they became convinced that Cassidy had not been killed. In 1910 the Bolivian government eventually filed an inquest and death certificates for the two American bandits "whose names were unknown." After examining the facts of the San Vicente shootout in 1913, William A. Pinkerton concluded that there was little truth to the notion that it was Cassidy and Longabaugh who were gunned down. As late as 1921 the Pinkertons believed that Longabaugh was in jail in Peru for bank robbery and that Cassidy was still at large somewhere in Argentina.

During the time Cassidy and Longabaugh lived in Argentina, Percy Seibert was a foreman of a large mining operation. In time the two fugitives went to work at the mines and became friends with Seibert. The three men grew to know one another well, and Cassidy often told the foreman of his desire to leave his outlaw days behind him and begin a new life where he wasn't known.

Following the shootout in San Vicente, Seibert traveled to the village and identified the American victims as Butch Cassidy and the Sundance Kid. It is, in fact, Seibert's identification that ultimately led many to believe the two outlaws finally met their end in Bolivia. Years later when Seibert was working as an attorney in South America, he reflected on his identification of Butch and Sundance, remarking only that if the law believed the two men were dead then perhaps they would end their pursuit and the two fugitives would be free to start over somewhere else.

It is a fact that there is no official record of the death of Butch Cassidy.

Relatives and friends of Butch Cassidy have stated repeatedly that the former leader of the Wild Bunch returned to the United States from South America, often visited with family members, and searched for and retrieved train robbery loot that had been hidden years earlier.

Other reports and rumors that have circulated throughout the West have Cassidy dying in Vernal, Utah, during the 1920s, in Oregon in 1930, in Mexico in 1932, in Chile in 1935, in Denver in 1936, in Tombstone, Arizona, in 1937, and in Nevada during the 1940s. According to relatives and a few researchers, a man believed to be Butch Cassidy used an alias, lived in Spokane, Washington, and died in 1937.

Lula Betensen Parker, the youngest sister of Butch Cassidy maintained that the outlaw returned to Utah in 1925 and spent some time visiting his family. She stated that Butch told relatives that the law was convinced he was dead and that he wanted to keep it that way. Betensen said Cassidy, after returning to the United States, spent much of his time trapping and prospecting in Alaska, Washington, and Wyoming. She agreed with the claim that Butch died in Spokane in 1937. She also stated he was buried in a secret location known only to a few family members.

Some who have researched the evidence that Butch Cassidy may have retuned to the United States where he allegedly lived for another two decades are convinced that Spokane resident William T. Phillips may have been the outlaw.

Phillips, an owner and operator of a machine shop, proved to have an unusual intimacy with the activities and personnel of the Hole-in-the-Wall Gang. During his later years he penned a manuscript that suggested he might have been the famous outlaw. A number of Cassidy's acquaintances that were still alive during the 1930s supported Phillip's contention, but others suspected he might have been a fraud.

While it may never be proven that Phillips was Butch Cassidy, the Spokane resident continues to baffle researchers for several reasons:

- He was able to relate stories and events that could only have been known to Cassidy and intimates.
- He was about the same age as Cassidy, assuming the outlaw was still alive at the time.
- At least one handwriting analysis concluded that William T. Phillips and Butch Cassidy were the same man.

Research has revealed that Phillips was an interesting and perplexing character. A skilled machinist, he is credited with inventing the garage door opener and the adding machine. His life is filled with mystery, and even those scholars who do not agree that Phillips was the famous outlaw admit to some difficulties discounting the possibility that there may be something to the claim.

After Phillips passed away in 1937, his widow told investigators that her late husband had, in fact, known Butch Cassidy during the late 1800s, but that he was certainly not the famous bandit. Both cursory and computer analyses of the facial features of Phillips and Cassidy suggest they were two different men. Researchers note that Phillips claimed he had undergone plastic surgery in order to change his appearance, but experts are doubtful.

Unfortunately the relationship between Phillips and outlaw Cassidy has never been subjected to statistically valid photo-comparison studies such as the one undertaken with Billy the Kid and William Henry Roberts (see chapter 1, "The Mysterious 'Death' of Billy the Kid").

The evidence for William T. Phillips being Butch Cassidy is intriguing, but until such time as something more substantial comes along, the claim must be evaluated with caution. On the other hand, the evidence that Cassidy did, in fact, return from South America to the United States where he remained until his death is compelling and difficult to dismiss.

How and where he lived and died and under what circumstances remain unsolved mysteries.

NINETEEN

・◆◆◆・

The Disappearance of
Harvey "Kid Curry" Logan

One of Butch Cassidy's close companions and fellow Hole-in-the-Wall Gang member Harvey "Kid Curry" Logan acquired a reputation as one of the West's better-known outlaws. As a truly bad man, Logan was a much deadlier outlaw than Cassidy, for unlike Butch, Curry was a killer.

Harvey Logan probably killed more men than any of his Hole-in-the-Wall companions. He was sometimes referred to as "the executioner" of the Wild Bunch, being responsible for perhaps one-third of all of the killings attributed to that famous gang of train robbers and cattle rustlers.

Existing records suggest Logan was killed in a shootout with lawmen near Parachute, Colorado. Some detectives present at the shooting who were acquainted with Logan, however, insisted the dead man was someone else. Pinkerton Detective Agency files have yielded surprising information that Logan, like Butch Cassidy and the Sundance Kid, escaped to South America where he resumed his career of robbing and killing.

A rumor eventually reached the United States that Logan had been killed in South America during a disagreement with one of his fellow outlaws. Other stories emanating from that continent contradict this tale and suggest Logan may have retired from outlawry and settled down to ranching. Unfortunately, there exist no facts to substantiate any of these positions. For all intents and purposes, Harvey Logan seems to have disappeared.

Harvey Logan was born in Kentucky during the early 1870s. Like many young men of his day he was convinced grand and glorious opportunities awaited him in the frontier West. As soon as he was able, he left Kentucky and, after many weeks of wandering, landed in Wyoming.

Logan was smaller than most of his companions, standing around five feet seven inches tall and weighing about one hundred and forty pounds. His dark hair, dark eyes, and well-groomed full mustache made him attractive to women, whose company he never lacked. When in the presence of ladies, Logan was described as always "charming," "polite," and "reserved."

One of the first opportunities presented to Logan in Wyoming was stealing cattle. Logan, along with several other men, joined with noted rustler George "Flat Nose" Currie. Under the tutelage of Currie, young Logan soon became a skilled livestock thief.

Around the same time, Harvey Logan became an accomplished killer. He was described by the Pinkerton Detective Agency as "cold-blooded" and "desperate." Despite Logan's aforementioned charm,

Harvey "Kid Curry" Logan and Annie Thayne. Annie Thayne (aka Maud Walker and Annie Rogers) was rumored both to have had a child with the Sundance Kid and to have wed Harvey Logan. See chapter 20.
Source: Library of Congress, Prints & Photographs Division, LC-DIG-ppmsca-07624

detective William Pinkerton once said of him, "He is the only criminal I know of who actually does not have one single good point." Today, Logan would be regarded as little more than a psychopathic killer. Butch Cassidy once stated that Kid Curry was the bravest man he ever saw.

As often happens when an area is overrun with cattle rustlers, neighboring ranchers grew frustrated and disgusted with the constant loss of stock and took matters into their own hands. A posse of ranchers finally caught up with George Currie and his gang. A number of the ranchers, angered at their losses, wanted to hang the cattle thieves on the spot and eliminate the rustling problem once and for all. The majority of them, however, were a bit squeamish about executing their prisoners without a trial. After some discussion, the ranchers talked Currie and his followers into signing an agreement wherein they would thereafter leave Wyoming cattle alone. Given the choice between signing the document and hanging, Currie, Logan, and the other rustlers scrawled their signatures or X onto the document. Soon afterward they were escorted under guard to the Nebraska state line and warned never to return.

Convinced that their futures lay someplace other than Wyoming, the outlaw gang disbanded. Young Logan eventually made his way into Montana where he adopted the nickname "Kid Curry" in honor of his cattle-rustling mentor.

On December 24, 1894, while living in Montana, Kid Curry killed a United States deputy marshal in front of at least a dozen witnesses. His subsequent escape took him back to Wyoming, and in a short time he arrived at the Hole-in-the-Wall where he assumed a leadership position and resumed his robbing and killing.

When lawmen began closing in on the gang, Kid Curry, along with several others, left for Arizona. In Clifton, Logan and accomplice Ben Kilpatrick robbed a bank of over $12,000. Following a dramatic escape where he jumped his horse across a wide arroyo, Logan fled eastward to Georgia. During the months following his arrival in Savannah, Logan spent money lavishly and at one point even vacationed in France.

In spite of the pleasures of his newfound lifestyle, Logan grew bored with the trappings of Georgia society and longed for more of the adventure he had found in the West. Before much more time passed he was back in Utah and reunited with several of his Wild Bunch companions. This time he was joined by his younger brother, Lonnie.

Shortly after arriving in Utah, Logan masterminded the robbery of a Union Pacific train. Using tactics he learned from Butch Cassidy, Logan dynamited open the express car safe and escaped with $30,000.

Confident they had made an effective escape, Logan and the gang were unaware they were being pursued by dozens of lawmen. Three days following the robbery, a posse rode in on the outlaws one morning as they were preparing breakfast in camp. During the ensuing gunfight, it is believed Logan shot and killed Sheriff Joe Hazen. With one of their leaders dead, the lawmen retreated.

The outlaws decided they should split up and go their separate ways, at least until the law lost interest in them. Unfortunately for the outlaws, local sheriffs, federal agents, and Pinkerton detectives remained dogged in their pursuit. One afternoon lawmen spotted Lonnie Logan entering an outhouse. After the door was closed, the officers quietly approached the structure and fired their weapons into it until they were certain the young outlaw was dead.

When Logan learned about the killing of his brother he seethed with anger and hungered for revenge. Within a few weeks he began engineering another train robbery. The attempt was successful, but the take was only fifty dollars.

Eventually Logan decided it was time once again to leave the Utah-Wyoming area. While detectives searched for him, he fled to Knoxville, Tennessee. Believing he was safe from pursuit, Logan was enjoying a drink in a local tavern when he was suddenly surrounded by police officers. While he was being arrested, Logan broke free, ran up the stairs to the third story, leaped out of a bedroom window, and escaped into the night. Unfortunately he didn't flee far enough and was captured two days later. He was tried, convicted, and sentenced to 130 years in the penitentiary.

As he was being readied for transfer to prison, Logan escaped once again, this time traveling west toward surroundings with which he was more familiar. Desperate for money, he soon formed a small gang and quickly returned to his outlaw ways.

In early June 1904, a Denver and Rio Grande train was robbed near Parachute, Colorado, and lawmen were convinced the perpetrators were Kid Curry and his gang. By now detectives had grown experienced in chasing train robbers and in a very short time they were mounted and armed and following the trail of the outlaws. The lawmen pursued and eventually caught up with a band of men believed to be those responsible for robbing the D&RG train. A brief gun battle ensued. One of the presumed train robbers, believed to be Harvey

Logan, took a defensive position behind some rocks and shot it out with lawmen while his companions escaped. When the officers finally overran the hiding place, they found the outlaw dead, shot through the head apparently by his own hand.

A few historians have deduced that Logan took his own life rather than be captured and sentenced to prison. The Pinkertons, along with D&RG detective R. Brunazzi, examined the body of the dead man and identified it as Kid Curry solely on the basis of a letter found on the corpse. The letter was addressed to Tap Duncan, one of Logan's several aliases. For the lawmen, the matter was closed and Harvey Logan was officially listed as dead. The body was subsequently buried at Glenwood Springs.

Other law officers involved in the chase, however, insisted the dead man was not Logan at all, but instead some minor outlaw they had occasionally encountered in the past. On the basis of a Texas postmark, the letter was eventually traced to its origin at Knickerbocker, Texas, where it was discovered it had been mailed to a man whose name was, in fact, Tap Duncan.

Though the official position of the Pinkerton Detective Agency was that Harvey "Kid Curry" Logan was killed, the embarrassed detectives renewed their pursuit of the elusive outlaw. In 1907, they encountered information that suggested Logan, like Butch Cassidy and the Sundance Kid, had fled to Argentina. In fact, some are convinced that Logan joined Butch and Sundance in South America for a time, even assisting them in at least one bank holdup.

Newspaper accounts have been found that indicate Logan, after arriving in Argentina, formed his own gang and conducted a series of robberies throughout Patagonia. According to Buenos Aires journalist Justo Piernes, on December 29, 1909, a man identified as Harvey Logan, along with two accomplices, robbed a mercantile company in Chubut Province, killing a clerk in the process. Several other robberies followed, most of them resulting in killings.

Newspaperman Piernes reported that, as time passed, the members of the Logan gang began feuding with one another and that Kid Curry himself was eventually shot down by one of his own companions in Chile. Thus far no evidence has been found to substantiate this tale, and to date it comes under the heading of speculation.

Other rumors suggest Logan retired from outlawry and settled down to ranching in either Chile or Argentina. Again, no one knows for certain. The fate of Harvey Logan, aka Kid Curry, one of the most notorious killers of the American West, continues to puzzle historians.

TWENTY

The Strange Case of Etta Place

One of the most enduring mysteries of the American West concerns the enigmatic figure we know as Etta Place. Who was she? Where did she come from? And what became of her? Though research into Etta Place has been extensive and ongoing, we still know very little about her, and most of what we know is suspect and fraught with contradiction. Even the name—Etta Place—was likely not her own.

Etta Place would probably amount to little more than a minor, if not practically unknown, figure in Western history were it not for the fact that she was a boon companion to the famous outlaws Butch Cassidy and the Sundance Kid. The truth, however, appears to be that even without that important association, Etta Place was still a rather colorful character and a woman of deep mystery.

The so-called historical records pertaining to the woman (or women) known as Etta Place have, in large part, been responsible for a great deal of the confusion surrounding this engaging and curious woman. Furthermore, the existing history, such as it is, has been subjected to a variety of diverse interpretations by different researchers, each offering different perspectives. The problems with the history of Etta Place begin with her origins. One story identifies her as the illegitimate daughter of a British Earl.

George Capel, who occasionally went by the alias George Ingerfield, was believed to have been the illegitimate son of the Sixth Earl of Essex, Arthur Algernon Capel. To avoid the real and potential embarrassment of the illegitimacy, baby George was given to be raised to Richard Boyle, Ninth Earl of Cork. As he grew to manhood, young Capel somehow managed to make enough enemies for himself and Boyle that he was encouraged to leave England. He went to America and made his way to the frontier West.

While visiting New York on one occasion, Capel met a woman named Emily Place, a distant relative, it is said, of Harry A. Longabaugh, later to become known as the Sundance Kid. Capel and Place became intimate, and she became pregnant. Capel abandoned her and returned to the West. The resultant child was a girl named Etta. Learning of the existence of his daughter, Capel, it is believed by some, subsequently made arrangements for the child to be raised by one Fannie Porter, a San Antonio, Texas, madam. Porter allegedly raised young Etta, sending her to some of the finest schools in the East. It was while visiting her benefactor in Texas in 1900, according to one tale, that Etta met and fell in love with the Sundance Kid.

Though they don't differ markedly, there exist several versions of the above story. None of them, however, are supported by any documentation whatsoever.

Sometime during the 1980s, a man claiming to be Harry A. Longabaugh Jr., the son of the Sundance Kid and a woman named Annie Thayne, came forth and made national headlines with his story. The alleged offspring of the famous outlaw provided a new and somewhat different perspective on Etta's origins. Similar to the previous tale, this one identified Etta Place as Laura Etta Ingerfield, daughter of George Ingerfield, aka George Capel. At Fannie Porter's house, according to Longabaugh Jr., a young Etta met Butch Cassidy, who took her with him back to Utah and placed her in the home of a Mormon family named Thayne to be raised. As she grew up in the Thayne household, Etta changed her name, or had it changed, to Ethel (some say Hazel) Thayne. One of Etta's foster sisters, Annie, became romantically involved with the Sundance Kid, the result supposedly being Harry Longabaugh Jr. Annie remained hopeful that she and Longabaugh Sr. would eventually wed, but while pregnant with Harry Jr., she was stunned to learn that the Sundance Kid had married foster sister Etta.

Longabaugh Jr. claimed he was in the possession of legal documents that supported his contentions, but as far as is known they were never seen by anyone but him. Though some are supportive of the notion that this claimant was who he said he was, credible researchers do not take his story seriously.

In her biography of Etta Place, Gail Drago relates a few odd and somewhat convoluted turns to the junior Longabaugh's tale. When Butch Cassidy, the Sundance Kid, and a few other members of the Wild Bunch arrived in Texas at the turn of the century, they encountered Annie and the baby. By this time, Annie was going by the name Maud Walker, and there is some evidence she also used the alias Annie Rogers. It has also been suggested that Annie Thayne aka Maud Walker aka Annie Rogers married Wild Bunch member Harvey "Kid Curry" Logan (chapter 19, "The Disappearance of Harvey 'Kid Curry' Logan").

Author Kerry Ross Boren offers yet another version. He claims Annie and Sundance rekindled their romance after meeting in Fort Worth, and that it was Annie, not Etta, who went to New York City and Argentina with the outlaw in 1901. Etta, says, Boren, did not go to Argentina until 1905. As proof, Boren claims to be in possession of Etta Place's memoirs. Boren's findings have been questioned by credible scholars who, at this writing, await definitive proof.

In a self-published book, Doris Burton advances the notion that Etta Place was actually a woman named Ann Bassett. Burton claims Bassett often used the alias "Etta Place" and offers the opinion that at least five other women did too. In what some regard as an extreme stretch of logic accompanied by no substantiation, Burton also claims that Bassett was one of three women in South America with Butch Cassidy and the Sundance Kid who used the name Etta Place. Burton opines that Longabaugh convinced all of these women to use the alias to confuse pursuing lawmen.

Burton does point out that Bassett, in her memoirs, never once claimed to be Etta Place, and most who have examined Burton's analysis suggest there exists no compelling evidence to cause anyone to believe she was. On the other hand, a photograph of Ann Bassett looks remarkably like the only known photograph of Etta Place. Both women were about the same size—five feet three inches tall and 110 pounds. They each had medium dark hair and blue or gray eyes. Both manifested a distinct heart-shaped face and possessed an identical hairline. Both women apparently possessed the same kind of personality, education, and bravado. Burton claims that a computer analysis of the two photographs suggested Etta Place and Bassett were the same person, but this has never been statistically verified.

Though the evidence for Ann Bassett being Etta Place is intriguing, few researchers have been willing to accept it as truth. One of those who resists doing so is Donna Ernst, a relative of Harry Longabaugh. Ernst offers a number of important inconsistencies that have yet to be successfully contradicted by Burton or anyone else.

Another story maintains that Etta Place was Eunice Gray, a Fort Worth prostitute. That conclusion was arrived at by newspaperman, Delbert Willis. The only tangible link between Gray and Place in Willis's account was that both women were in South America at about

The Sundance Kid and Etta Place.
Source: Library of Congress, Prints & Photographs Division, LC-
USZ62-132506

the same time. There is little else in the story that would cause one to
suspect Gray and Place were the same. Research into the matter has
failed to provide any support for Willis's claim.

At least one other account claims Etta Place's actual name was Amy Parker and that she was a cousin to Butch Cassidy. Amy Parker, claimants say, was born in Kanosh, Utah, in 1879. Photographs of Amy Parker reveal a striking resemblance to Etta Place.

Other theories abound. One suggests that the Sundance Kid and Etta Place were brother and sister. One researcher offers the theory, based on questionable evidence, that Etta Place was a schoolteacher somewhere in the East and met the Sundance Kid during a visit to Texas.

Yet another version claims Etta was an unemployed San Antonio music teacher named Ethel Bishop. In need of money, Bishop allegedly went to work at Fannie Porter's San Antonio establishment and, while there, met the Sundance Kid. Research has revealed that an Ethel Bishop was a resident of San Antonio at the time and that she apparently disappeared from the city around the same time Etta Place left for New York with Harry Longabaugh. Other than that interesting coincidence, detailed substantiation is lacking.

Despite the many versions of her history, the facts about the origin of Etta Place remain obscure. There may be a bit of truth in each of the foregoing accounts. Just as likely, however, there may be none at all.

Whatever and whoever Etta Place was, there exists some agreement, according to the Pinkerton Detective Agency, that she was "refined." Their files indicate that she may have been a schoolteacher and that her subject may have been music. Depending on which account one prefers, Etta Place taught in Massachusetts, Denver, and/or Texas.

Though several researchers suggest Etta Place was born in Denver, the Pinkertons were convinced she was from Texas. Longtime Pinkerton employee Frank Dimaio, who spent thousands of hours in pursuit of Cassidy, Longabaugh, and Place both in the United States and South America, claimed to have been in possession of evidence that indicated Etta's parents were from Texas.

Etta Place may or may not have been a prostitute. Some historians have tried very hard to link Etta with Fannie Porter's house of ill repute in San Antonio, but straightforward evidence in support of this claim does not exist. The notion that Place may have been a prostitute comes largely from a statement made by Butch Cassidy to Percy Seibert wherein he stated that "She was the best housekeeper on the Pampas, but she was a whore at heart."

Etta Place may not have been her real name. The name "Place" can be found in the genealogy of Harry Longabaugh—his mother's maiden name was Place. In fact, Longabaugh often went by the alias Harry A.

Place. According to the Pinkertons, there exists no evidence that Etta
Place ever used the name Etta until she moved to South America with
Sundance. Up until that time, she was known by the names Ethel,
Ethal, Eva, and Rita. Pinkerton detectives have opined that Etta may
have been a Spanish or Portuguese pronunciation or corruption of the
name Ethel.

Most researchers are reasonably certain that near the end of 1900,
Etta and the Sundance Kid rode a train to New York. There, it is believed, they were married, although no record of the union has ever
been found. It has also been speculated that the couple then took a
train to Sundance's boyhood home in Pennsylvania where he introduced Etta to family members as his wife.

From Pennsylvania, the couple traveled to Buffalo, New York, arriving in January 1901. Here, they checked into Dr. Pierce's Invalid
Hotel. It has long been assumed that Longabaugh admitted himself
to the hospital to receive treatment for pain and aggravation from an
old leg wound and/or catarrh, an infection of the membranes of the
nose and throat, a condition that bothered him for years. Why Etta
was admitted is open to conjecture. There is evidence that she suffered
from a chronic appendix problem, but those who are committed to the
proposition that she was a prostitute have jumped to the conclusion
that she may have been suffering from venereal disease. Furthermore,
Dr. Pierce's Invalid Hotel was well known around the country as a
place to go for the treatment of syphilis. The hospital closed down
during the 1940s and no records are known to exist.

Following their stay at the hospital, the two honeymooned at Ni-
agara Falls and then traveled to New York where they met Butch
Cassidy. In New York, Etta and Longabaugh went by the name of Mr.
and Mrs. Harry A. and Ethel Place. Here, she introduced Cassidy to
her brother, James Ryan. This has caused a few researchers to suspect
that she and Butch may have been related.

It was in New York where Etta and Sundance posed for what many
refer to as their wedding picture. It is the only photograph of the
woman called Etta Place known to exist.

On February 20, Etta and Sundance boarded the S.S. *Herminius* for
Argentina. It is believed that Cassidy returned to Montana around this
time, robbed a train, and some time later joined Etta and Sundance
in Buenos Aires.

While researchers have looked long and hard for information on the
activities of Etta, Sundance, and Cassidy together in South America,

details remain sketchy. It is a fact, however, that Cassidy and Long-abaugh filed on government land in the Province of Chubut in western Argentina near the Chilean border. The land was fertile, and several successful ranching operations could be found there. At the first opportunity, the two outlaws intended to purchase land to raise, cattle, horses, and sheep.

Butch Cassidy and the Sundance Kid remained in the area for approximately four years, living as law-abiding ranchers and businessmen. Eventually, however, they returned to their outlaw ways. Some say they did so because they ran out of money. Others suggest they simply missed the adventure. It is believed that Etta, wearing men's clothing, aided them on at least two bank robberies.

Etta's residence in South America, like the rest of her life, remains a mystery. During her stay in Argentina with Butch Cassidy and the Sundance Kid, it is believed that she returned to the United States on at least two, and perhaps three, occasions. Various explanations have been offered for these journeys, including homesickness and the need for medical attention. In 1906 Butch Cassidy told his friend Percy Seibert that Sundance had taken Etta to Denver for an appendectomy. Another reason given for her return to the States was that she required treatment for venereal disease. Yet another version of the story has Etta, now pregnant, returning to the United States to have her baby.

It was rumored that the baby was not Longabaugh's, but rather the result of a liaison between Etta and one of their Argentine neighbors, a man named John Gardiner. Gardiner was deeply in love with Etta, and the two spent a great deal of time together. At the same time, Gardiner despised Longabaugh and never believed he treated Etta appropriately. According to one researcher, Etta, after returning to the United States, gave birth to a girl she named Flora Jane. The same source says she never returned to South America.

What became of the woman known as Etta Place? No one knows. Even today some rumors persist that she was killed along with Butch and Sundance during a robbery attempt. The Pinkertons maintain she was alive and living in Argentina with Longabaugh in 1907. At least one Pinkerton informant claimed he viewed the bodies of Cassidy, Longabaugh, and Place after they were killed during a bank robbery attempt in the town of Mercedes in 1911.

According to biographer Drago, one story has Etta growing old in the United States, bearing several children, and finally passing away in 1966 close to the age of ninety. Another tale has her committing suicide in 1924. A more bizarre story has Etta Place leading a successful gang of bank robbers during the Depression Era. Drago relates yet another rumor wherein Etta and Sundance are thought to have reunited in the United States and ran a successful scam operation in Tacoma, Washington. Still another story, also reported by Drago, has Etta marrying an Irishman, a politician, or a fight promoter, and moving to Paraguay, where she gave birth to two daughters. A report buried deep in the files of the Pinkerton Detective Agency states that Etta Place was shot and killed in Chubut Province in 1922.

Perhaps one of the most intriguing stories places Cassidy, Longabaugh, and Place in Mexico during the Revolution, fighting alongside Pancho Villa. Interestingly, Cassidy relatives who maintain the outlaw survived to return to the United States and live to be an old man claim he did, in fact, join Villa's forces during the early 1900s. There exists no evidence to support any of the above suppositions.

So, who then was Etta Place? Where did she come from? And what became of her? The ultimate truth is that no one knows the answer to any of those questions.

TWENTY-ONE

The Missing Head of Pancho Villa

Today in Mexico, nearly a century after his assassination, the name Pancho Villa continues to evoke admiration and awe among the poor and disenfranchised, the citizens of that country for whom the famous general fought. Numerous tales continue to swirl around this legendary bandit-turned-revolutionary, a man who led his army into battle in the fight for the rights of the peasants.

Even during his lifetime, the many tales told about Villa strained credulity. With his death they may have grown even more fantastic. Villa's numerous biographies relate almost unbelievable adventures, escapades, escapes, battles, and romance. They are the stuff of dreams for most mortals.

As amazing as his life was, Pancho Villa's death and the subsequent related events are even more bizarre. The heroic Mexican had been buried for only two and a half years when his body was disinterred in the dark of night and his head stolen. To this day, no one knows for certain who perpetrated the deed or why, and the present location of the head of Villa, the most famous of all Mexican bandits and generals, remains unknown.

Pancho Villa was born Doroteo Arango in the Mexican state of Durango. An oft-told legend repeated by his biographers states that after he became a successful young cattle rustler and bandit, he adopted the name Pancho Villa. The original Villa was a noted bandit and apparently served as an important influence to his namesake. Another version of how he got his name was offered by Emil Holmdahl, who knew the bandit well and served for a time as a mercenary in his revolutionary army. Holmdahl once stated that Villa himself told him that his real father, named Arango, was killed. His mother subsequently married a man with the surname Villa.

Pancho Villa.
Source: Library of Congress,
Prints & Photographs Division,
George Grantham Bain Collec-
tion, LC-DIG-ggbain-36806

According to another legend, Villa was about sixteen years old when he was forced to become an outlaw. He was helping to support his family by working as a sharecropper for a wealthy *hacendado* when this event occurred. On returning home from the fields late one afternoon, he learned that the son of the *hacendado* had raped his younger sister, Maria. After obtaining a pistol, young Villa searched for and found the son and killed him with a shot to the head. Knowing that he would likely be put to death for his deed, Villa fled into the nearby mountains and commenced his life as a bandit. Soon afterward, stories circulated about a band of outlaws stealing cattle, horses, and gold from the wealthy landowner and distributing much of the booty among the peasants. The outlaws were led by a man who went by the name of Pancho Villa.

When the idealistic Francisco Madero decided to oppose reigning Mexican president Porfirio Diaz and fight for peasant rights, Villa and his men joined him. Madero eventually pardoned the bandit for all of his past crimes and awarded him the rank of colonel in the Army of the Revolution.

For ten long years Villa fought against the Mexican government. His guerilla raids and battles cost the *federales* tens of thousands of lives and untold tens of millions of pesos. In 1920, government officials decided it would be cheaper to buy off the now famous and much idolized revolutionary leader than to continue to fight him. Villa was offered a 25,000-acre ranch in Durango along with 500,000 pesos and a paid retinue of fifty men on the condition that he cease his opposition to the government.

Villa, suffering from several wounds and, it is believed by some, from syphilis, had by this time grown weary of the war and readily accepted the offer. He disbanded his ragged army and moved onto the ranch with one or more of his wives. The once mighty guerilla leader now raised cattle and crops and managed the fortunes of the thriving enterprise. On Saturdays, Villa and selected friends would travel into the nearby town of Parral for an evening of reveling.

On Saturday, July 19, 1923, Villa, accompanied by a half-dozen of his famed *dorados*, drove his large Dodge touring car into Parral. The men visited cantinas and whorehouses until they collapsed from exhaustion during the early morning hours.

After the sun had been up for a short time, Villa roused his followers, telling them it was time to return to the ranch. After seeing his charges loaded into the Dodge, Villa took the wheel, started the engine, and steered the huge car through town.

Near the edge of Parral, Villa slowed the Dodge in order to negotiate a sharp turn in the road. As he did, rifle fire spat from the cover of a nearby building, bullets ripping into the driver and the passengers. Within seconds, all were dead. It is believed Villa was killed instantly. He had been struck in the head and nearly one dozen times in the body. Following the initial fusillade, according to one version of the attack, a man wearing a straw hat walked out of a nearby building, drew a revolver and, placing the barrel against Villa's forehead, fired another shot. After holstering the pistol, he calmly walked away.

With very little ceremony, Pancho Villa was buried in the tiny cemetery just outside of town. At the head of his grave family members erected a wooden cross bearing his name.

Why Villa was assassinated and by whom has never been clear. Some researchers ascribe the motivation to Mexican government officials who were responding to rumors that the bandit leader, now forty-six years old, was considering a run for political office. Fearing that Villa would trouble anew the waters that had become relatively calm during the previous two and a half years, some are convinced emissaries of the government arranged for the assassination. Following the Mexican Revolution, there was no shortage of men who were anxious to kill Villa.

Many believe the assassin—or more accurately, the leader of the group responsible for the killing of Villa and his men—was Jesus Salas Barraza. Barraza was a politician of relatively high standing in Parral, and shortly after the killing he admitted culpability. His reason, he claimed, was that he despised Villa, whom he said took and raped his younger sister and allowed his soldiers to use her. Through their neglect, Barraza said, his sister later died while giving birth to a baby.

Barraza's confession was accepted without question and the case was officially closed. He was sentenced to the Parral jail but released in less than one year. Many of those who have researched the circumstances of Villa's assassination are convinced Barraza was in league with high-ranking government officials who likely arranged for his short sentence.

Late in the evening of February 5, 1926, two and a half years following the assassination, a person, or perhaps a small group of men, entered the quiet Pantheon Cemetery near Parral. In the dark of night, the body of General Pancho Villa was dug up and the head taken. According to Villa scholar Haldeen Braddy, that same night a group of five men placed the head atop a long pole and carried it through the streets of Parral.

Sometime during the night of the fifth or the morning of the sixth of February, a small airplane landed at the Parral airstrip located a short distance from the cemetery. As the plane waited at the end of the runway with the engine running, two, maybe three, men approached it and handed a package inside. In turn, something was handed to them and they departed. Minutes later the plane taxied down the runway and rose into the dark sky.

Around dawn on the morning of February 6, cemetery caretaker Juan Amparan was walking among the headstones when he made a grisly discovery. The hastily disinterred body of Villa was lying in the open amid the shattered ruins of his wooden coffin. Approaching the body, the caretaker shuddered when he noticed the head was missing.

Amparan ran into town and reported his discovery to the mayor. A short time later, policemen arrived at the site to investigate the disinterment. The only things they discovered that could possibly be considered as evidence were a tequila bottle containing residue that smelled like antiseptic, wads of cotton, and drops of blood. The presence of the blood was puzzling, for it could not have come from a body that had been buried for two and a half years. Perhaps, they surmised, one of the grave robbers was injured during the act. When word of the desecration spread, curiosity seekers arrived and many carried off pieces of the coffin and even parts of the body.

Barraza was an immediate suspect, but subsequent investigation revealed his presence that night had been accounted for. Since the assassination, Barraza had been under constant police surveillance.

In a matter of a few short weeks a bizarre story circulated throughout northern Mexico: Villa's head was removed because, it was said, beneath his hair was a tattooed map showing several locations of buried treasure in the Sierra Madres. While a provocative tale, the story bears an astounding resemblance to a Greek myth. To date, no one has been able to prove or disprove this contention.

Within a few days following the grave robbery a number of suspects were identified. One was Sam Dreben, known as "The Fighting Jew." Dreben had been a mercenary and fought in the Boxer Rebellion as well as in Guatemala and Honduras. He arrived in Mexico during the Revolution and immediately found work. On several occasions, Dreben skirmished against Villa's forces. It is believed Dreben became a suspect because he had a high profile and because he was regarded as one of very few men with the courage to undertake the job of stealing Villa's head. Suspicion of Dreben was short-lived, however, when it was learned he had died almost a year prior to the theft.

A more likely suspect was Tracy Richardson, another American mercenary who fought against Villa in 1912. It was well known that Richardson despised Villa, and it would not have surprised his acquaintances to learn he had stolen the head. At the time of the disinterment, however, it was explained that Richardson was employed as a surveyor near the Mexico-Guatemala border, well over one thousand miles away. His actual presence there during the time of the robbery, however, has never been officially established.

According to writer Douglas V. Meed, El Pasoan Larry A. Harris received information in 1932 that Richardson, fleeing from Mexican police, arrived in El Paso with Villa's head. According to the informant, Richardson was to collect $10,000 for the trophy. Richardson decided to hide the head until he received the money. It is believed he buried the head in a secret location somewhere in the nearby Franklin Mountains. Whether the head was ever retrieved by Richardson or anyone else was never learned. While a few claim that Richardson could not have stolen the head, the former mercenary has never been completely eliminated from suspicion.

Another suspect was Mexican general Francisco R. Durazo. Writer Elias Torres advanced the notion that one of Villa's opponents during the Revolution, a high-ranking officer, offered a handsome reward for the head of the bandit. While Torres never provided a name, many believe Durazo was the officer in question. Torres contended that the mysterious airplane that landed near the cemetery the night of the grave robbery may have contained this officer, or was at least ordered to the site by the same man. According to Torres, the head of Villa was delivered to the officer by the man or men who stole it, and it sat on the officer's desk for many years, a grisly trophy for the vengeance-minded military leader. At the time he wrote of this, Torres provided no identity for the mysterious officer and similarly offered no evidence for his contention.

The story of the airplane and the military officer appears again in Mexican history and folklore. Señora Luz Coral Villa, one of Villa's widows, provided the name of an officer she believed was responsible—General Francisco R. Durazo. In addition, Durazo was implicated by Mexican historian Oscar A. Martinez. At the time of the grave robbery, Durazo was a brigadier general in charge of the military garrison at Parral.

Shortly after the disappearance of Villa's head, stories appeared in several U.S. newspapers that the robbery was orchestrated by a wealthy Chicago resident who intended to turn the head over to a researcher for study. Dr. O. F. Scott, identified as a Chicago brain surgeon, was quoted as saying he expected to receive the head any day and that he looked forward to examining it. Almost immediately, incensed representatives of the Mexican government demanded the immediate return of the head. Embarrassed U.S. officials confessed they knew nothing of the theft, and a spokesman for the American Medical Association stated that from a scientific standpoint the head was worthless. Whether Dr. Scott ever received the head is unknown.

Another suspect, and one that continues to intrigue investigators today, was Emil Holmdahl. With considerable mercenary experience in the Philippines and Central America, Holmdahl, originally from Iowa, eventually came to Mexico to fight in the Revolution. In Mexico, Holmdahl gained recognition for his skills and abilities with machine guns and heavy artillery. During the time he commanded Villa's military forces, Holmdahl was promoted to the rank of colonel. In 1913 Holmdahl and Villa began to disagree on tactics, and the mercenary resigned and enlisted in the army of General Alvaro Obregon, a man who was despised by Villa.

In 1916 Holmdahl was arrested for illegally transporting guns and ammunition into Mexico and sentenced to a prison term. A short time later, Villa and his forces raided Columbus, New Mexico, and the U.S. government sent General John J. "Blackjack" Pershing in pursuit. From prison, Holmdahl contacted Pershing and volunteered to serve as scout. The general quickly arranged for his release.

During what became known as the Punitive Expedition into Mexico in pursuit of Villa, Holmdahl was allegedly offered $10,000 to kill the bandit general. During a 1962 interview, Holmdahl stated that the offer was made to him by General Bell at the behest of Colonel Herbert Slocum and General Pershing. Slocum had been in command at nearby Camp Furlong during the Mexican raid on Columbus. The money, according to Holmdahl, was to come from Russell Sage, the millionaire father-in-law of Slocum. According to the mercenary, the offer was made to him because Bell and Pershing believed he was the only man who could get close enough to Villa to assassinate him. Holmdahl was told that Colonel Slocum considered the raid on Columbus an insult to his honor, "and the only way this blot could be removed was by the death of Villa."

It has long been suspected that there was collusion between Villa and the U.S. government relative to the Columbus raid, collusion specifically involving Villa, Pershing, and Slocum. Researcher and writer Bill McGaw has suggested that Pershing and Slocum wanted Villa dead in order to guarantee his silence.

In the end, Holmdahl refused the offer to assassinate Villa, claiming he was incapable of such a thing. Those who knew Holmdahl well, however, maintain the mercenary was completely capable of killing anyone, anytime. During a 1962 interview when Holmdahl was seventy-nine years old, he stated he turned down the offer for three reasons. "First," he said, "I am not an assassin. Second, I liked the guy. And third, I would have never gotten out alive."

While some disagree about Holmdahl's involvement in the theft of Villa's head, the evidence for him as the culprit is compelling. First of all, Holmdahl was in Parral on the evening prior to the beheading. Second, in Holmdahl's automobile, police found a bottle containing a small amount of some liquid they later identified as embalming fluid. Holmdahl maintained it was only mineral water. Third, in the mercenary's hotel room police found an axe with relatively fresh blood on the blade. Fourth, on the afternoon of February 5, Holmdahl was reported to have asked for directions to the location of Villa's grave. Fifth, his whereabouts between 8:00 PM and 11:00 PM on the same day were in question.

Holmdahl was arrested and taken to the police station for questioning. He told the investigators he was in the employ of the American Smelting and Refining Corporation and was in the area prospecting for signs of copper. His claim was never officially verified.

While some researchers suggest the axe may have been employed to break open Villa's coffin, Holmdahl claimed he used it to kill an animal in the woods on the previous day.

The next morning at Holmdahl's hearing, the bottle allegedly containing embalming fluid was presented as evidence. Holmdahl restated that it contained only mineral water. Seizing the bottle, he raised it to his lips, drank the entire contents, and slammed it down on the table. He then told the judge that if it had been embalming fluid it would have killed him. Impressed by Holmdahl's defense, the judge dismissed the charge.

The evidence against Holmdahl was to accumulate over the years. In 1957, L. M. Shadbolt, a former mercenary himself and friend of Holmdahl, wrote a letter to noted Villa researcher Haldeen Braddy of El Paso. In 1927 or 1928, according to Shadbolt, he and a friend named Clyde Creighton were staying at El Paso's Sheldon Hotel where Holmdahl was a resident. One evening, says Shadbolt, Holmdahl entered their room carrying "a bundle wrapped in newspaper under one arm and a bottle of Don Jose Cuervo under the other." Holmdahl then told Shadbolt and Creighton he had something to show them and, "holding one edge of the newspaper wrapping his bundle, he gave a casual flip and out rolled General Villa's head." According to Shadbolt, Holmdahl told them he was to be paid $5,000 for the head by the Cassell Institute in Chicago. According to what Braddy learned, Holmdahl was never able to deliver the head.

Holmdahl is also closely linked to the alleged tattoo of a treasure map or maps on Villa's head. A number of researchers are convinced Villa hid millions of dollars' worth of gold and silver in various locations in Mexico and the United States. Most of Villa's treasure has never been recovered. In 1952, the United States Secret Service undertook an investigation into a mysterious cache of gold ingots somewhere in the American Southwest, a cache allegedly worth twenty million dollars and believed to have been buried by the Mexican general. Interestingly, the first person arrested in this case was Emil Holmdahl, and many believe that the former mercenary, using the map on Villa's head, located the fortune.

Holmdahl may have found other caches left behind by Villa. It was later determined that the former mercenary once transported a substantial number of gold ingots from Mexico to the United States.

During the several interviews Holmdahl was subjected to throughout his colorful life, however, he emphatically denied having a role in stealing Villa's skull and claimed he knew nothing of its whereabouts.

In spite of the heavy suspicion and the array of evidence associated with the contention that Holmdahl was the man who stole Villa's head, definite proof is lacking. During his last interview while he was living in Van Nuys, California, Holmdahl again insisted he had nothing to do with stealing the head. He had been guilty of many things during the time he was a mercenary, he said, but grave robbing was not one of them. He admitted he was in Parral at the time the head was stolen and that he had been arrested for the deed. He claimed, however, that anyone familiar with the case of Villa's stolen head knows he did not take it.

Mexicans are convinced that an American desecrated the grave of their hero, Pancho Villa. It is thus related in their *corridos* and poems. In the popular ballad, "The Beheading of Pancho Villa," it is sung:

> The gringos no longer respect
> Even the peace of the grave.
> They have desecrated the tomb
> Of Pancho Villa in Parral

The Mexicans, for the most part, believe Holmdahl was the culprit. In other verses of "The Beheading of Pancho Villa," scholars believe they are referring to Holmdahl when they sing:

> He broke the concrete
> With an iron crowbar
> And removing the loose earth
> He withdrew the corpse from the crypt
>
> And then cut the head
> Poor human remains
> And leaving the grave open
> The American fled

And where is the head today? Was it buried on the slopes of El Paso's Mount Franklin by Tracy Richardson? Was it used for a time as a trophy, displayed atop the desk of Mexican General Durazo? Is it now stored away in some dusty attic or cellar deep in Mexico? Or is it hidden among other specimens in some Chicago research facility?

According to Mexicans living in Parral, a ghost walks the nearby countryside. It is a headless apparition that is sometimes seen around midnight. They insist it is the ghost of Pancho Villa and that he is searching for his head. Others suggest the ghost of the general appears regularly to remind the peasants to continue to fight for what is rightly theirs.

¿Quien sabe? Who knows? Who knows what this ghost means? And who knows the location of Villa's head? We may never know.

TWENTY-TWO

The Aurora Incident

Fifty years before the so-called Roswell Incident wherein, allegedly, a spacecraft crashed in the New Mexico desert and yielded bodies of space creatures, helping enter into our vocabulary such terms as "unidentified flying object" and "alien," a similar incident occurred in Aurora, Texas.

Aurora is located just off U.S. Highway 287 not far from Fort Worth. Around 6:00 AM on the morning of April 19, 1897, according to an article in the *Dallas Morning News* penned by reporter E. E. Haydon, a strange craft, described as an "airship," sailed over the Aurora public square and continued northward toward the home and property of Judge J. S. Proctor. Flying low to the ground, the craft struck the judge's windmill, toppling it and destroying the adjacent water tank. A moment later, the craft exploded, scattering debris over several acres.

The newspaper article stated that the "pilot of the ship is supposed to have been the only one aboard and, while badly disfigured, enough of his remains had been recovered to show that he was not an inhabitant of this world."

Haydon goes on to relate that U.S. Army Signal Corps officer T. J. Weems provided the opinion that the pilot "was a native of the planet Mars," though how he would know such a thing is not clear. Papers found on the pilot contained writing that was described as "unknown hieroglyphics" and could not be deciphered. The craft, according to those who examined it, was constructed of some unknown metal "resembling a mixture of aluminum and silver, and . . . weighed several tons." It could not be determined what powered the craft.

The pilot of the ship was carried to the Aurora Cemetery and buried "with Christian rites." Today, a marker at the entrance of the cemetery provides some history as to its origin and the names of a few prominent citizens buried there. Near the end of the marker's information is found this sentence: "This site is also well-known because of a legend that a spaceship crashed nearby in 1897 and the pilot, killed in the crash, was buried here."

Most of the debris from the wreckage was gathered up and dumped into the well that was located beneath the windmill. A few of the pieces, it was learned, were buried with the alien in the cemetery. A few days later, military personnel visited Aurora and gathered up some of the remaining crash debris. They told residents they were going to analyze it but nothing was ever heard from them.

In 1945, Aurora resident Brawley Oates purchased Judge Proctor's property. Determined to use the old well as a water source, he cleaned out most of the metal fragments from the spacecraft that had been deposited there. Over time, Oates developed a severe and dramatic case of arthritis that he claimed resulted from drinking water that had been contaminated by the wreckage. In 1957, Oates sealed the well, covering it with a concrete slab over which he constructed a shed.

News of the Aurora incident did not travel much beyond the immediate area, and soon the matter was largely forgotten for nearly a century. In May 1973, a United Press International report revived the incident and described legal proceedings underway to exhume the body of the pilot of the craft.

A few days later, another UPI report quoted Mary Evans, a ninety-one-year-old resident of the town, who recalled the crash. She had been fifteen years old at the time and "had all but forgotten the incident" until it was revived in the newspapers. She recalled that her parents had gone to the site of the crash but insisted she remain at home. She recalled that the remains of "a small man" had been buried in the Aurora Cemetery.

Charlie Stephens, who was ten years old at the time, recalled seeing the slow-moving airship trailing smoke as it headed toward the town. He wanted to go see the crash but his father made him stay home and finish his chores. Later, his father, who went to see the wreckage, described it to him.

A short time later, an Associated Press report carried the information that a professor from North Texas State University had found some odd metal fragments near the Oates gas station, which was located on the old Proctor property. The professor said one fragment was particularly intriguing because it consisted primarily of iron but exhibited no magnetic properties whatsoever, and that it was "shiny and malleable instead of dull and brittle like iron."

The Aurora Cemetery Association has blocked all attempts to excavate the grounds in search of the alien. The actual location of the grave of the alien was not clear. A tombstone had been placed over the site years earlier but it had been stolen.

Over the years, unidentified pieces of metal have been found in the area, presumed by some to be debris from the craft. When word got out about the finds, according to some Aurora residents, military personnel appeared and confiscated the pieces.

A few contend the Aurora spaceship crash was a hoax. Barbara Brammer, a former mayor of Aurora, is one who questions the notion that an alien craft came down in the town. She stated that during the time of the alleged crash, the cotton crop, the major source of income for the town, had been devastated by a boll weevil infestation. A short time later, a fire on the west side of town destroyed several buildings and took some lives. Not long after this, an epidemic of "spotted fever" struck the area, "nearly wiping out the remaining citizens and placing the town under quarantine." Finally, plans for a railroad stop in the town were changed and the tracks bypassed Aurora. The town, claims Brammer, was in danger of dying out. As a result, reporter Haydon, who Brammer describes as a "bit of a jokester," wrote the spaceship crash article as a last ditch attempt to keep Aurora alive.

In a 1979 *Time* magazine article, Aurora resident Etta Pegues supported Brammer's contention that Haydon fabricated the entire event in order to "bring interest to Aurora." Pegues claimed there was never even a windmill on Judge Proctor's property.

During the early 2000s, an investigative team arrived at the cemetery with the goal of disinterring the body of the pilot of the airship that had been buried there. According to their report, they "uncovered a grave marker that appeared to show a flying saucer of some sort." Using a metal detector, they recorded strong readings from something immediately below the marker. The team requested permission to excavate the site and exhume the body and any pieces of metal but were denied.

A short time after the visit by the investigators, the marker disappeared and a three-inch pipe was placed into the ground at the site. A subsequent visit to the site by the team yielded no metal readings from the grave. It was presumed that whatever had been buried there had been removed since their last visit.

In 2008, Tim Oates, current owner of the property where the spacecraft crashed, allowed investigators to unseal the well and examine any debris they might find below. Water drawn from the well was tested and it was found to contain a high concentration of aluminum. No metal debris was found in the well, and Oates explained that a previous owner of the property had all of the metal removed. The remains of the base of a windmill were found nearby, which refuted the earlier statement by Etta Pegues that there was never a windmill on Judge Proctor's property.

The Aurora incident has been investigated by dozens of people, written about, featured numerous times on television, and even made into a movie. Most who have spent time studying this event rule out the notion of a hoax; definitive evidence for such does not exist.

On the other hand, what actually happened at Aurora in 1897 is not entirely clear. If it had been a clear attempt at a hoax, the occasional appearance and involvement of military personnel would not have been warranted. Furthermore, the evasive responses and clear tampering associated with the so-called alien grave create suspicion.

What happened in Aurora in the early morning of April 19, 1897? No one seems to know for certain.

Selected References

Airy, Helen. *Whatever Happened to Billy the Kid?* Santa Fe, NM: Sunstone Press, 1993.

Albano, Bob (Ed.). *Arizona Highways: Days of Destiny.* Phoenix: Arizona Highways, 1996.

Arnot, Richard D. "Bandit Queen Belle Starr," *Wild West*, August 1997.

Balsiger, David, and Sellier, Charles E. *The Lincoln Conspiracy.* Los Angeles: Schick Sun Classic Books, 1977.

Bates, Finis L. *Escape and Suicide of John Wilkes Booth, Assassin of President Lincoln.* Memphis, TN: Pilcher Printing Company, 1907.

Betenson, Lula Parker. *Butch Cassidy, My Brother.* Provo, UT: Brigham Young University Press, 1975.

Braddy, Haldeen. *Mexico and the Old Southwest.* Port Washington, NY: National University Publications, 1971.

———. "Who Stole Pancho Villa's Head?" Unpublished manuscript in the Braddy Collection, University of Texas at El Paso Library.

Bryan, George S. *The Great American Myth.* New York: Carrick and Evans, 1940.

Burns, Walter Noble. *Tombstone: An Iliad of the Southwest.* New York: Doubleday and Company, 1927.

Burrows, Jack. *Johnny Ringo: The Gunfighter Who Never Was.* Tucson: University of Arizona Press, 1987.

Crutchfield, James A., O'Neal, Bill, and Walker, Dale L. *Legends of the Wild West.* Lincolnwood, IL: Publications International, 1995.

Curry, George (Ed. H. B. Henning). *George Curry, 1861–1947: An Autobiography.* Albuquerque: University of New Mexico Press, 1958.

Dajani, Laika. *Black Bart: Elusive Highwayman-Poet.* Manhattan, KS: Sunflower University Press, 1996.

Drago, Gail. *Etta Place: Her Life and Times with Butch Cassidy and the Sundance Kid.* Plano: Republic of Texas Press, 1996.

Drago, Gail, and Ruff, Ann. *Outlaws in Petticoats and Other Notorious Texas Women.* Plano: Republic of Texas Press, 1995.

Earp, Josephine Sarah Marcus. *I Married Wyatt Earp: The Recollections of Josephine Sarah Marcus Earp* (Edited by G. Boyer). Tucson: University of Arizona Press, 1976.

Eisenschiml, Otto. *In the Shadow of Lincoln's Death.* New York: Wilfred Funk, 1950.

Faulk, Odie B. *Tombstone: Myth and Reality.* New York: Oxford University Press, 1972.

Fergusson, Erna. *Murder and Mystery in New Mexico.* Albuquerque: University of New Mexico Press, 1971.

Garrett, Pat F. *The Authentic Life of Billy the Kid.* Norman: University of Oklahoma Press, 1954.

Gibson, A. M. *The Life and Death of Colonel Albert Jennings Fountain.* Norman: University of Oklahoma Press, 1965.

Hardin, John Wesley. *The Life of John Wesley Hardin as Written by Himself.* Norman: University of Oklahoma Press, 1961.

Harkey, Dee. *Mean as Hell.* Albuquerque: University of New Mexico Press, 1948.

Hornung, Chuck. "The Fornoff Report: New Light on the Death of Pat Garrett." *True West*, March, 1998.

Jameson, W. C. *Lost Mines and Buried Treasures of the Guadalupe Mountains.* Clearwater, FL: Garlic Press, 2011.

——. *Legend and Lore of the Guadalupe Mountains.* Albuquerque: University of New Mexico Press, 2007.

——. *Lost Treasures in American History.* Lanham, MD: Taylor Trade Publishing, 2006.

——. *Billy the Kid: Beyond the Grave.* Dallas, TX: Taylor Trade Publishing, 2005.

——. *New Mexico Treasure Tales.* Caldwell, ID: Caxton Press, 2003.

——. *Return of Assassin John Wilkes Booth.* Plano: Republic of Texas Press, 1999.

——. *Buried Treasures of Texas.* Little Rock, AR: August House, 1991.

——. *Buried Treasures of the American Southwest.* Little Rock, AR: August House, 1989.

Kelly, Charles. *The Outlaw Trail: The Story of Butch Cassidy.* New York: Bonanza Books, 1959.

Knowles, Thomas W., and Landsdale, Joe R. (Eds.). *The West That Was.* New York: Wings Books, 1993.

Kyle, Thomas G. "Computer, Billy the Kid, and Brushy Bill." *True West*, July 1990.

Lake, Stuart N. *Wyatt Earp: Frontier Marshall.* Boston: Houghton Mifflin Company, 1931.

Las Cruces Sun News. "New Mexico Residents Claim Billy the Kid Died in Ramah." June 17, 1989.

Meadows, Ann. *Digging Up Butch and Sundance.* New York: St. Martin's Press, 1994.

Meadows, Ann, and Buck, Daniel. "The Last Days of Butch and Sundance." *Wild West*, February 1997.

Meed, Douglas V. "Who Stole Pancho Villa's Head?" *True West*, August 1996.

Metz, Leon Claire. "Strange Death of Pat Garrett." *Wild West*, February 1998.

——. *John Wesley Hardin: Dark Angel of Texas.* El Paso, TX: Mangan Books, 1996.

——. *The Shooters.* El Paso, TX: Mangan Books, 1976.

——. *Pat Garrett: The Story of a Western Lawman.* Norman: University of Oklahoma Press, 1974.

Moore, Jack E. "The Mystery of the Fountains." *Wild West*, February 1998.

Myers, John Myers. *Doc Holliday*. Lincoln: University of Nebraska Press, 1955.

Owen, Gordon R. *The Two Alberts: Fountain and Fall*. Las Cruces, NM: Yucca Tree Press, 1996.

Poe, John W. *The Death of Billy the Kid*. Boston: Houghton Mifflin Company, 1933.

Pointer, Larry. *In Search of Butch Cassidy*. Norman: University of Oklahoma Press, 1977.

Read, Benjamin M. (Ed.). *Illustrated History of New Mexico*. Chicago: Lewis Publishing Company, 1895.

Schweidel, David, and Boswell, Robert. *What Men Call Treasure: The Search for Gold at Victorio Peak*. El Paso, TX: Cinco Puntos Press, 2008.

Shirley, Glen. *Belle Starr and Her Times*. Norman: University of Oklahoma Press, 1982.

Skarren, Warren. "Pancho Villa's Last Gasp." *Texas Monthly*, December 1983.

Sonnichsen, C. L. *Tularosa: Last of the Frontier West*. Albuquerque: University of New Mexico Press, 1960.

Steele, Phillip. "Eddie Reed—Belle Starr's Son," *Quarterly of the National Association for Outlaw and Lawman History*, July–September 1997.

———. *Outlaws and Gunfighters of the Old West*. Springdale, AR: Heritage Publishers, 1991.

Walker, Dale L. *Legends and Lies: Great Mysteries of the American West*. New York: Forge, 1997.

Wilson, John Francis. *John Wilkes Booth: Fact and Fiction of Lincoln's Assassination*. Boston: Houghton Mifflin, 1929.

Wilson, Lori Lee. "Although Born to One of the Wild West's Most Notorious Couples, Ed Reed Makes Good in the End." *Wild West*, August 1997.